THE LOST FILM

THE LOST FILMS FANZINE, VOL. 1, #3 FALL 2020

EDITOR AND PUBLISHER: JOHN LEMAY SPECIAL CONSULTANT: KYLE BYRD SPECIAL THANKS THIS ISSUE TO DANNY LEE BEANE, JOEY PALINKAS, MAXWELL BRESEE, ERIC ELLIOTT, LEE POWERS, STEVEN SLOSS, RAFFAEL CORONELLI, DAPHNESHARD AND STAN HYDE

THE LOST FILMS FANZINE IS PUBLISHED FOUR TIMES A YEAR. THE COPYRIGHTS AND TRADEMARKS OF THE IMAGES FEATURED THEREIN ARE HELD BY THEIR RESPECTIVE OWNERS. THE LOST FILMS FANZINE ACKNOWLEDGES THE RIGHTS OF THE CREATORS AND THE COPYRIGHT HOLDERS OF THE IMAGES THEREIN AND DOES NOT SEEK TO INFRINGE UPON THOSE RIGHTS. ALL TEXT COPYRIGHT THE RESPECTIVE AUTHORS OF THE ARTICLES.

of this fanzine that you've ever seen, not every issue is all monsters all the time. But this one is. Issues usually aren't 100 pages long either, but I felt a monster-themed issue might as well be monster-sized. Therefore, this issue covers all the greats in some capacity—especially the classic monsters like Frankenstein, Dracula, the Wolf Man and the Mummy (sorry Gilman, just didn't have room this issue!).

Growing up, I naturally saw the black and white Universal classics. But, for a kid in the 90s they were a tad outdated. What really caught my eye were the Hammer films. My first introduction to Hammer was probably one of those old horror trailer compilation VHS put out by Goodtimes Home Video. The previews I caught on that tape (which I don't recall the name of) certainly made an impression on me, but what sealed the deal in terms of my love for Hammer was catching a quick glance at *Brides of Dracula* on Sci-Fi Channel. I was struck by the technicolor and the action. Specifically, I caught the scene where one of the titular brides is coaxed out of a fresh grave. Not long after, Peter Cushing is attacked by a giant bat.

To me, this was far more exciting than the old Universal films (though I certainly still liked them). *Brides of Dracula* sent me into a Hammer frenzy, inspiring me to track down every single entry that I could find on VHS. And this being the 90s, these were the pre-Amazon days. Some of them, *Legend of the Seven Golden Vampires* (1974), in particular, were tough to track down. But the entire year of 1998 I must've seen dozens of Hammer films for the very first time. It's a year that I still look back fondly upon for that very reason. And each year thereafter, I would do my best to track down a new Hammer I had yet to see (again, pre-Amazon days here). Today, I'm pleased to say there's still a few Hammer horrors I have yet to see (looking at you *Dr. Jekyll and Sister Hyde* and *Horror of Frankenstein*). Maybe this year I'll finally get around to them...

NEWS

Superman's black suit cut from *Justice League* (left), and Ben Affleck, Gal Gadot and Zack Snyder during filming (right). Justice League © 2017 Time Warner/DC Comics

THE SNYDER CUT COMETH

In 2016, during filming of *Justice League*, director Zack Snyder had to step down from the film due to the tragic death of his daughter. Despite the fact that the film was nearly finished, Warner Bros took this as an opportunity to retrofit the picture into something tonally more akin to *The Avengers* (2012). As it was, many fans had been displeased with the dark tone of Snyder's *Batman v Superman* (2015), as so the studio brought in Joss Whedon to finish the film with a lighter touch. Though Whedon added some great bits into the film, tonally the result was a bit of a mess. Not only did it not match the previous two films in the DC Cinematic Universe, the movie felt like it was directed by two different people... because it was. When the film was released in November of 2017, only about one fourth of Snyder's footage remained as Whedon reportedly added about 80 pages of new material to the script. Nor was the film terribly well-received. And, despite the backlash he received on *Batman v Superman*, many fans began clamoring to see the Snyder cut of *Justice League*.

Eventually, a large amount of vocal fans petitioned for the Snyder cut to be completed. Happily, in May of 2020, Snyder revealed that his cut of *Justice League* would be completed for exclusive streaming on HBO Max sometime in 2021. At the moment, the plan is to air the cut in either six episodes, or a four-hour director's cut. "It will be an entirely new thing, and, especially talking to those who have seen the released movie, a new experience apart from that movie," Snyder told *THR*. $30 million will be spent in post-production to make it as close to Snyder's original vision as possible. This will include scenes with Superman donning his post-resurrection black suit, which was one of the most hyped aspects of the Snyder cut.

It will be interesting to see if this becomes the definitive version of the film which usurps the theatrical version.

The best and most lyrical writing he has ever done.
...Don't miss it.
—Develope
Rich Dedre

Richard Brautigan

author of
The
Abortion

the hawkline monster

A Gothic Western

NEWS BRIEFS

CHANGES TO INDY V Here's what might be our first instance of COVID-19 necessitating script changes. For starters, the pandemic delayed production by an entire year, but reportedly it has also slightly altered the script.

Frank Marshall told Collider, "The number one thing, obviously, is the safety of everybody -- the cast, the crew, and all of us... You won't see a lot of big crowd scenes, for example, for a while." Nothing major, really, but interesting nonetheless.

STEVEN KING DOES JASON This past summer, Steven King tweeted some details on a non-existent project that sounded like a horror fan's dream. On June 14 he said, "The best novel idea I never wrote (and probably never will) is I JASON, the first-person narrative of Jason Voorhees, and his hellish fate: killed over and over again at Camp Crystal Lake." King followed it up with another tweet reading, "Just thinking about the legal thicket one would have to go through to get permissions makes my head ache. And my heart, that too. But gosh, shouldn't someone tell Jason's side of the story?" Me thinks King is actually trying to generate some interest in the project. After all, why wouldn't the owners of Jason want King drumming up some new blood for them?

HAWKLINE MONSTER FINALLY FILMING? Ever since the novel, *The Hawkline Monster* by Richard Brautigan, was published in 1974, reports of a film version have surfaced from time to time. I saw the project reported in the 1970s issues of *Famous Monsters* several times, and one rumor even had Jack Nicholson attached.

The novel is a gothic western set in 1902 that "tells of two unlikely hero gunslingers hired by a 15-year-old girl named Magic Child to kill the monster that lives in ice caves under the basement of a house inhabited by a young woman named Miss Hawkline. What follows is a unique adventure where there is more to Magic Child, Miss Hawkline and the house than meets the eye."

As of right now, Yorgos Lanthimos (*The Favourite*) is slated to direct, Tony McNamara (also *The Favourite*) will script, and New Regency will produce.

JAPANESE EVIL DEAD FINALLY GETTING A RELEASE *Bloody Muscle Body Builder in Hell* began shooting in 1995 under director Shinichi Fukazawa. It was finally

Deleted scene from *Batman Forever*
© 1995 Time Warner/DC Comics

finished in 2005, and now 15 years later it will see a DVD release in the U.S. via Wild Eye Releasing. The story concerns a bodybuilder trapped in a haunted house and has been nicknamed the "Japanese Evil Dead."

BATMAN FOREVER **EXTENDED CUT?** Due to both the looming *Justice League* redux and the ='passing of director Joel Schumacher, there's been talk of his extended 170-minute version of *Batman Forever* (1995). This darker version of the film delved more deeply into Bruce Wayne's psyche and had a dream scene of him fighting a giant bat. Among other deleted scenes were Two-Face escaping from Arkham. If the footage still exists, and if the *Justice League* cut continues to generate publicity, there's a chance this long lost cut might be resurrected. All that said, there's nothing concrete

from Warner Bros on this at the moment.

JELLYFISH EYES 2 **A NO GO** COVID-19 has claimed another film in the form of *Jellyfish Eyes 2*. Producer creator Takashi Murakami announced the cancelation on his Instagram account on June 30 stating that his company is facing bankruptcy due to the pandemic.

DOBKIN REVEALS ORIGINAL PLANS FOR KING ARTHUR TRILOGY David Dobkin, the original director of *King Arthur: Legend of the Sword* (2017, directed by Guy Ritchie) recently revealed his original plans for the film, which he envisioned as the first of a trilogy. He cast *Game of Thrones* Kit Harrington as King Arthur, with Joel Kinnaman as Sir Lancelot. The two actors shot a screen test which Warner Bros international department didn't like for some reason, and insisted the leads be recast. On top of that, Dobkin's original script was rewritten by Joby Harold. Once he saw it, Dobkin became uninterested in returning. Considering the completed film was something of a failure, perhaps Dobkin's version would have fared better.

WEREWOLF **FINALLY GETTING HOME VIDEO RELEASE?** *Werewolf* (1987-88) was one of the first series ever broadcast on the Fox Network and ran only one season. It has never seen a home video release. The closest it ever came was a release from Shout! Factory in 2009 which was shelved due to difficulties with music rights. Rumor has it that Mill Creek is about to release the long lost series.

BEWARE OF *BEWARE! THE BLOB!*

by Danny Lee Beane

The 1972 film *Beware! The Blob* is a unique counterculture experience. For a film that is definitely a product of the hippie era, this film is decidedly anti-counterculture, featuring many scenes played for laughs at the expense of the hippies. It is a schlocky experience that can be loved by low budget horror genre aficionados and loathed by more mainstream film enthusiasts. How am I, a reviewer, supposed to properly review this film? When you look at the threadbare plot, mediocre acting, and almost amateur cinematography, it is a terrible film worthy of at best a D rating. However, for fans of B movie trash, there is an almost schizophrenic charm to this trainwreck of a film.

When the Blob awakens, the movie turns into a delightfully devilish series of gore-filled vignettes with only the most minimal plot or character development connecting them. The cinematography has all the charm of a student project shot on 16mm film. The acting mostly consists of improvised guest appearances of famous comedians at the time. For such a low budget film, the special effects hold up surprisingly well as people get devoured by the Blob. There are even some fairly convincing miniatures of a bowling alley at the end of a film.

The movie opens up with the film's most sympathetic character, a fluffy kitten frolicking among flowers, to a hilariously ridiculous song accompanied by random screams. We are then introduced to Chester, an oil pipeline technician back from spending three months working on a project in the arctic. One thing you will immediately notice about Chester that stands out is his love for indoor camping as he immediately heads to his tent set up in the living room. I also appreciate his love for drinking beer out of empty flower vases. Seriously, if I enjoyed anything half as much as this man appreciates drinking beer, I would be a much happier, more relaxed member of society.

Various Lobby Cards for *Beware! The Blob.*

then Marianne, and then in a truly horrifying scene, Chester. Our new protagonist, Lisa is introduced. A friend of Chester and Marianne, Lisa walks in on Chester being blobbed. In a panic, she drives off to find her boyfriend Bobby. The rest of the film is just a series of vignettes of people being killed by the Blob until it feels like the producers ran out of money.

Some of the more entertaining scenes are as follows.

-A Turkish guy in a fez taking a bath who escapes the blob by throwing a telephone out a window and fleeing down a road at night naked.

-An uncomfortable scene of a hippy paying $400.00 for a hair cut by a barber... I mean hair sculptor.

-Hippies being un-necessarily threatened by a cop ending with a mandatory "Watch out behind you!" scene.

-The main character that is obsessed with avocado sandwiches. (See avocado is not just a millennial food!)

A piece of the Blob that was dug up by a bulldozer in the arctic was brought home by Chester to be analyzed. His wife Marianne opens up the container causing the Blob to thaw out and awaken. To steal a line from Prometheus, the much better movie involving deadly goo, "Big things have small beginnings". The Blob's rampage starts with it absorbing a fly. From the fly, it moves on and consumes a kitten,

-Guest appearance by Burgis Meradith, and the film's director Larry Hagman as a couple of transients hanging out on a chicken farm.

Speaking of Larry Hagman, this film was directed by Larry Hagman (pre-*Dallas* and post-*I Dream of Jeanie* fame.) Throughout his long acting career, Larry Hagman also directed many popular TV episodes.

Beware! The Blob, however, was his only foray into feature-length films. The producer of the original *The Blob*, Jack H. Harris, had been trying to get a sequel off the ground for years. Larry Hagman was his neighbor and admitted that he had never seen *The Blob*. A private 16mm screening later and *Beware! The Blob* had its director.

According to Wikipedia (one of the only places I could find information on this film), most of the cast consists of friends and neighbors of Hagman who were asked if they wanted to be blobbed. There were several big-named comedians at the time that had cameos in the movie. Though they appeared on the advertising, only Godfrey Cambridge and Dick Van Patton received any significant screen time (and Van Patton was killed off-screen!)

The best scenes of *Beware! The Blob* are any scenes featuring the spfx. *Beware! The Blob* featured a marginally higher budget than the original film. The Blob, for the most part, is fairly convincing, instead of using dyed silicon, as was used in the original, the blob goo was made with a special powder mixed with water. One of my favorite SPFX moments is when you see a 3rd person point of view of the blob moving around and it is clearly a silicon-coated drum spinning in front of the camera. I really got a kick out of that Blob-vision. Also, anytime the Blob devours someone, you are in for some gory goodness. The death of Chester was probably the most horrifying effect in the

film. The final confrontation in the bowling alley at the end of the film also featured some excellent use of miniatures. The only shots that looked cheap were the shots of a clear tarp illuminated with a red light meant to portray the Blob.

My main complaint against this film is the dialogue. Most of the

VHS release under the *Son of Blob* title. The box art highlights the numerous guest stars.

dialogue in this movie is improvised so most of the characters come off as rambling idiots. Marianne has some of the most pointless dialogue I've ever heard in a movie with a scene of her speaking to her cat while preparing its food. It just keeps going on and on. My favorite dialogue from her is "You broke my 49 cent thing. I really did like that thing!" The creepy scene with the hippie getting his hair cut by the

Robert Walker Jr. was the look alike son of his famous father, Robert Walker Sr. His mother asked Larry Hagman if he could have a role in the film and Hagman obliged. With him is Gwynne Gilford.

hairstylist was another scene that comically seems to go on forever. I believe that everything in this movie was filmed in one take. That's the only way to explain the terrible improvised dialogue.

The last bit of information I would like to talk about is whether or not this is actually a sequel to the movie *The Blob!*, or if it's a sequel to events that happened in the film and inspired a movie called *The Blob!* I bring this up for mainly two reasons. At the beginning of the movie, Chester is watching *The Blob* in his living room. This is clearly an anachronism put in a gag. The second reason is if *The Blob* almost destroyed the town and was airlifted to the Arctic, you would think it would have all sorts of warning signs and security around it. So how did an oil pipeline technician dig up a chunk of it with a bulldozer? All I know is that it's probably not worth my time to think about it. With this paragraph, I've probably put more thought into the timeline of this movie than all

this movie's filmmakers combined.

I would not recommend this movie for the vast majority of the people out there. It has pacing issues with the long drawn out dialogue. The plot of the movie is threadbare at best. Most of the characters are unlikable and the logic at times makes no sense. The cinematography is also amateurish. Despite all the film's shortcomings, there is value in this movie for the fans of B movie trash. The gore effects are certainly worthy of viewing. This movie is also weird in the sense that it is so bad it almost feels like an avant-garde art piece and starts to be good again. It just has this weird pacing that at times feels like an experimental film. The people that would get the most value out of this are people that want to watch dumb movies with their friends while enjoying a few drinks and just want to riff the movie to pieces. As one of the people that enjoy making fun of bad movies, I most definitely recommend it for that purpose.

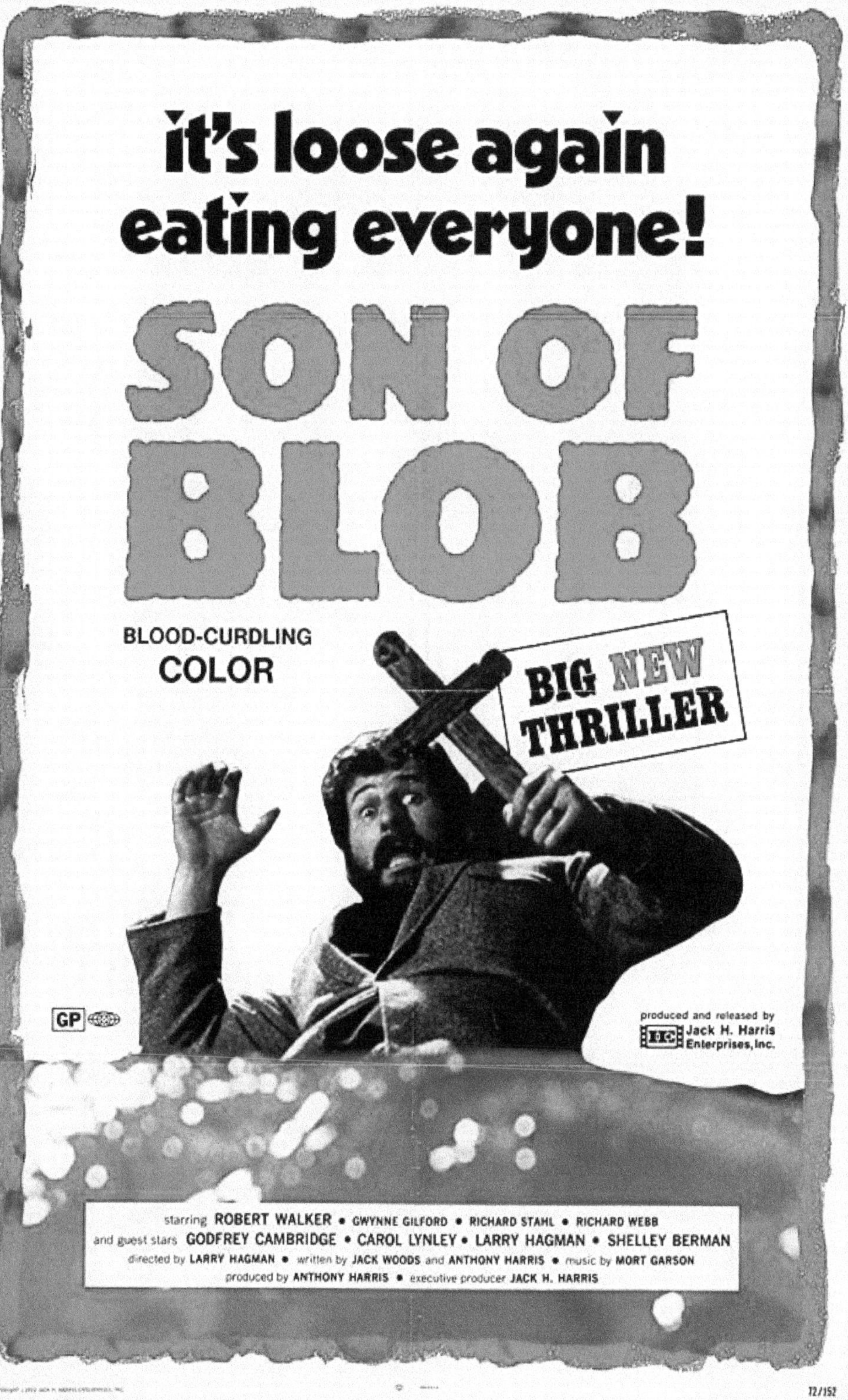

72/152

"SON OF BLOB"

THE BLOBS THAT WEREN'T

You would think that a monster as well-known as the Blob would've spawned more sequels—made and unmade alike—than it ultimately did. As of right now, 1958's *The Blob* produced the Seventies sequel just covered by Danny Lee Beane and a 1988 remake and that's basically it. Notice I said basically. Naturally, there are a few unproduced sequels to *The Blob*, its sequel, and its remake, plus a few other forgotten Blob-related projects you've probably never heard of before...

Before we get to those, let's talk about the origins of the Blob itself. Supposedly, the Blob is said to have been partially inspired by a real-life UFO encounter. Eight years before the movie was made, on September 26, 1950, two police officers, John Collins and Joe Keenan, were on their usual patrol in Philadelphia, Pennsylvania. Suddenly, a strange purple object floated across the beam of their headlights about half a block in front of them. They watched in amazement as the strange purple "what's it" landed in an open field. Naturally, they went to the landing site to investigate. There they found a purple domed disk composed of a quivering astral jelly that measured six feet in diameter!

At its highest point, the dome was one foot thick. Upon turning off their flashlights, the two policemen were shocked to see that it glowed with a strange mist. Odder still, the men felt that the strange substance was somehow alive. Not sure how to handle this odd, potentially harmful substance, they radioed for backup. They were soon joined by Sergeant Joe Cook and Patrolman James Cooper.

When the lawmen tried to pick up samples of the giant, Jell-O-like object, it began to fall apart. The bits that stuck to their hands began to evaporate. Thirty minutes later, the entire substance had disappeared.

This strange incident stuck in the mind of producer Jack Harris, who got the ball rolling on what would eventually become *The Blob* with writer Irvine H. Millgate.

The initial form for the blob was always the same, but with a few variations on its abilities. Millgate described it to Harris as a "monster never done before." He excitedly called Harris at 2:30 in the morning to tell him about his ideas for the monster, which he said could defy gravity by climbing trees. When dropped from great heights it would simply splatter and reform itself. Another ability he envisioned for the as of yet unnamed blob was the ability to "zap prey." If Millgate meant he envisioned it as having the ability to fire a ray, or simply reach out and grab its prey is unknown.

Proposed names for the monster included Lava, the Mineral Monster, the Mass, and as a potential film title, *The Molten Meteor*. As a joke, someone either suggested *The Glob that Gobbled the Globe* or *The Glob that Girdled the Globe*. Harris latched onto *The Glob*, and decided to give the film that title until he discovered it had already been used, hence *The Blob*.

As is usually the case in Hollywood lore, where everyone likes to take credit for good ideas and deny bad ones, I've come across some

conflicting reports on Blob sequels. In his autobiography, *Father of the Blob,* Jack Harris said that he never pondered a sequel himself, feeling that the first film had done everything it could with the concept. Instead, the first sequel pitch came to Harris by way of Richard Clair, a high school English substitute teacher who was also a huge fan of *The Blob.* He essentially wrote a sequel/spoof entitled *A Chip Off the Old Blob.* At first Harris dismissed it as a "cute joke piece" until he saw Clair do a live comedy routine on stage. Clair, by the way, eventually caught the eye of Carol Burnett and was the mind behind her famous Mama's Family skits. Harris eventually read the *Chip* script, but ultimately disliked the fact that it was a spoof. If the blob returned to the silver screen, he wanted to do so in another straight forward horror pic.

As for some conflicting information (remember what I said about Hollywood), contrary to what Harris claimed about not believing in doing a sequel, in 1964 appeared an ad for *Son of Blob!* It appeared on November 2nd in the *Daily Variety,*

which reported that Harris was negotiating with Allied Artists to produce it. It also stated that the sequel would a widescreen-color production.

If IMDB's rather dubious trivia section is to be believed, a Blob TV series was also pitched before *Beware! The Blob* began to gestate. IMDB reports: "According to producer Jack H. Harris, there were at least two proposed television series based on this film. None had made it to the pilot stage. Harris jokingly suggested that The Blob could become a good guy and solve crimes." However, I can find no source for that information outside of IMDB.

What we do know for sure was that in the early 1970s Larry Hagman and Jack Harris were neighbors. One Sunday the duo were hanging out, which was unusual because Hagman had the odd habit of not speaking on Sunday, presumably as a way of letting his voice rest. He usually made no exceptions, and communicated via writing on a notepad. In fact, he wrote his desire to see *The Blob* on a piece of paper, to which Harris obliged. When the movie was over, Hagman broke his rule and spoke: "That f----n' movie still holds up. How come you never made a sequel?"

And that is how the ball got rolling on the Blob sequel. (An alternate story says Harris's son wrote the script beforehand and that Harris Sr. asked Hagman if he'd be interested in the production).

In his autobiography, Harris wrote that he reacquired Claire's *Chip Off the Old Blob* script and used that as the basis for what they were currently calling *Son of Blob,* but removed the spoof aspect. Reportedly before shooting, Harris had the cast and crew chant the following mantra: "*Son of Blob* shall be scary and not funny." They didn't listen.

The movie finished shooting in 1971, and was supposed to come out that Christmas. It was postponed to the summer of '72 because it was felt it would play better to a summer drive in audience.

The film played simultaneously as *Beware! The Blob* and *Son of Blob*, with the latter eventually emerging as the more popular of the two. It's unknown just how well the film did. It's likely that it generated a profit, but probably not as much as the Harris wanted. Apparently, Anthony Harris (Jack's son) wrote a sequel pitch called *Curse of the Blob* during shooting on *Son of Blob*. Its non-production is probably our best indicator as to how profitable *Son of Blob* really was.

Instead would come a Blob remake in 1988. Though Columbia executives loved it at a preview screening, and anticipated sequels, it was a flop at the box office. That same year, Harris was at it trying to make a comedy re-cut of the original Blob called *Blobermouth*! It was actually completed by Harris and shown at various film festivals in Europe!

Blobbermouth had no new footage to my knowledge, and was simply a re-dub of *The Blob*. The idea was that the Blob, given a mouth via animation, and Steve McQueen were rival comedians trying to get onto "The Tonight Show"!!!

While showing the film in Europe, Harris discovered that an Italian TV network had already been illegally using footage from *The Blob* to make its own comedy spoof. It was called *The Blob Show* and aired on the RAI Network. The program aired at 7:30 and mixed in bloopers from the news with footage from

The Blob. Harris caught an episode in stunned silence. He said that the episode he saw showed McQueen talking on the telephone, and on the other end was an angry Italian hooker! Harris ultimately won a $250,000 payment for copyright infringement.

Fourteen years later, in 2002, there was talk of another Blob remake. The project began gestating when Scott Rudin reached out to Harris about a Blob remake at Paramount. In discussing the deal with a friend, Jon Peters, Harris was swayed to take the remake idea to Warner Bros instead. This turned out to be a mistake, as Peters became distracted with getting a new Superman movie out and dropped the ball on *The Blob*, according to Harris in *Father of the Blob*. Harris contacted Bob Bissell of Warner Bros and got the ball rolling yet again.

Harris was supplied with a treatment he didn't particularly like, and a full screenplay he liked even less. Because of studio politics and rehiring among other things, the Warner Bros remake was dead by 2005.

But that wasn't the end of Blob remakes. Talks of a remake of Harris's 1959 feature *4-D Man* at Paramount again led to another possible Blob remake. This time Harris actually liked the script, and Paramount even took to his revisions and suggestions. But, due to the ever changing stable of Paramount staff, the Blob remake froze and died, again.

The next studio to approach Harris was Dimension Pictures in 2007. By 2009, Rob Zombie was attached to direct. By 2015, he was out, and Simon West was in.

Zombie's take on the story would have been quite a departure to the mythos. Concept art by Alex Horley showed people turned into Blob-Zombies of a sort, an interesting idea. Again, going just off the concept art, it would seem a monolith from space crashes in a small town and begins mutating people. I saw no images of an actual Blob, though that doesn't mean one wouldn't have come into play. So, essentially Zombie's version seemed to be The Blob creates zombies.

When Zombie exited the project he wrote,

"The Blob was going to happen. I was dealing with people on the movie, even though I was on the fence about doing anything that was considered a remake again. I really didn't like the idea of that, but just as I went down the road further with the producers and the guys that owned the property, I didn't feel good about the situation and I just walked away from it. My gut told me this was not a good place to be."

The 2015 iteration of *The Blob* from West and Goldcrest Films may still be gestating, we're not sure. Back in 2015, they gave the following logline on the story: "When a band of miners uncover something hidden deep beneath the earth they unwittingly unleash a hideous creature beyond imagination. Now the townsfolk must fight back, before it destroys everything."

That same year West said, "With modern CGI we can now fully realize the potential of *The Blob*. The world I create will be totally believable, immersive and emotionally satisfying. It's a thrill to introduce an enduring icon to a wider audience and a whole new era of fans."

According to remarks he made to Screen Relish, his take seemed to be just as different as Zombie's. He said,

"It's going to be much more sci-fi than the original. It's a bigger scale type of movie. It's more Alien meets Predator and designing the creature is a long and involved process cause its very sophisticated. It's not going to be the goo pouring through windows. So, that's taking a while to design and construct that."

The movie was supposed to start shooting in August of 2015, and the last we heard of the film was 2017, when West teased its production once again. Considering that was three years ago, and we now dwell in the land of COVID-19, chances of the Blob coming back to movie screens remains bleak for the foreseeable future.

By the 1950s, the "Classic Monsters" established by Universal were basically dead as far as new productions went.[1] The old Gothic Monsters were out and had been supplanted by aliens and mutants, not unlike Universal's own Gillman from *The Creature from the Black Lagoon* (1954). The last time Universal had utilized its classic monsters was only to serve as fodder for *Abbott and Costello Meet Frankenstein* (1948).

But then, in 1957, came Hammer studios with *The Curse of Frankenstein*. Shot in technicolor with bosoms and blood, it was a far cry from the 1930s and 40s Universal horror films.[2] And audiences loved it.

Having found success with Frankenstein, Hammer naturally turned their attention to Bram Stokers *Dracula*. There was one problem, however; *Dracula* was not yet in the public domain. As Bram Stoker had died in 1912, and being that it took 50 years for a work to fall into the public domain, *Dracula* would not be up for a copyright-free remake until 1962. Therefore, Hammer struck a deal with Universal to adapt the film, with Universal getting to distribute the film as an added bonus (later, Universal would agree to let Hammer remake their classic library of monster movies including *The Mummy*).

Jimmy Sangster, the writer for *The Curse of Frankenstein*, was instructed to adapt Stoker's novel and not Universal's 1931 film. Whether this is because the film was more or less a rather boring stage play, or because Hammer was not allowed to specifically emulate Universal's version, is up for debate.

In any case, Sangster was instructed to more or less keep it cheap. This eliminated some of the grander bits, such as Dracula traveling by ship to England, etc. and the action became more localized. As to the elimination of characters like Renfield, that was simply done because there was no room in the story's runtime (remember, back then movies often played as double features, meaning studios wanted each film to clock in at under 90 minutes).[3]

Fundamentally, Sangster's first draft script is the same as the finished film[4] aside from changed dialogue and a few deleted scenes, one of which occurs right after the credits roll.

First off, Sangster's version takes place in 1899, not 1885. Sangster's envisioned credit sequence says nothing of the castle backdrop in the opening shot, just dark clouds blocking out the sun so that the scene would only be colored in grey black and black grey. Otherwise, he does get in the bit about displaying the title by way of the coffin.

Sangster's first scene was either deleted or not shot in the first place, though the former is the more likely of the two options—we'll get to that later. As Sangster describes a carriage coming along a bend in the road, with a driver and a companion at the helm (a shot present in the film), we were to then cut to the inside of the carriage. There he reveals five passengers: Jonathon Harker and a priest on one side, and on the other a middle-aged husband and wife, and a "fat worried looking" merchant.[5]

Sangster makes it clear that this has been an uncomfortable ride for the passengers, who seem taught with the tension of an argument recently ended. Through the dialogue, it soon becomes apparent that the passengers are well aware of Harker's destination and have been doing their best to dissuade him from going to Castle Dracula.

The woman makes an appeal to Harker that if he has any loved ones then he dare not go for their sake, while her husband chides Harker as an "obstinate fool."

The priest then takes a turn. "I am a man of God my son. The words that I speak are words that I feel in my humble way, God might speak."

"If dissuasion is what you wish to speak then those will not be the words of God," Jonathon replies.

Greatly incensed, the male passenger exclaims, "Blasphemous too...mad and blasphemous."

Of course, the occupants have no idea that Jonathon is on a secret mission to destroy Dracula, in essence, God's work. Of course, nor would we, the audience, at this point, know this either had the footage been included.

Just as the carriage rolls to a stop, the priest indicates that the castle is the gate to Hell itself. The companion of the driver then pokes his head down through the window to ask Harker if he still wants to get off.

Harker affirms that he does, stands to thank the woman for her concern, and is then rudely pulled out of the carriage by the driver's companion. The fat merchant shouts for them to get away from the place as Harker's luggage is thrown at his feet. The carriage drives away as he looks on.

The film, as we all know, opens with a voice-over from Harker, and the first shot is of his diary. Harker explains recent events, and that he is on his way to Castle Dracula, in essence speeding up the action.

Even Sangster felt the V.O. was an improvement over the scene he had written. But once again we must ask the question, was the carriage scene filmed to begin with?

Director Terence Fisher was asked about this "deleted scene" by Gary R. Parfitt, and Fisher claimed that it was never filmed at all.[6] There is evidence to the contrary, however. The actors to play the parts were listed in both the British publicity folder for the film as well as Universal International's press sheet. They were as follows: Guy Mills (Coach Driver), Dick Morgan (Driver's Companion), Stedwell Fulcher (Man in Coach), Judith Nelmes (His Wife), Humphrey Kent (Fat Merchant in Coach), and William Sherwood (Priest in Coach).[7]

Sangster, on the other hand, speculated that the carriage scene was cut for budgetary reasons. In *Inside Hammer*, he writes, "I wasn't around at the time, but I imagine this change was made for budgetary reasons. A coach, possibly with back projection, five actors, half a day to shoot it...lotsa money. I see from an original cast line that all these parts were cast, so it was possibly the schedule that forced them to cut it."[8]

In the finished film, we do see one exterior shot of the carriage as it goes by. Two drivers sit at the helm, while four passengers are visible inside. If the exterior was shot with multiple people seen in the carriage, then perhaps the interior scenes were shot too?

Some film historians have also speculated that because the Universal *Dracula* had scenes of Harker within the carriage, that this would make the two films too similar. Remember, Hammer was not remaking Universal's *Dracula* as they would later do with *The Mummy*. In this case, Universal only

sold them the rights to adapt Stoker's novel.

In any case, in the film, Harker also seems to give an embittered look over his shoulder as he walks through the woods. Though the narration tells us that his coach driver wouldn't take him all the way, it's possible that actor John Van Eyssen was reacting to the previous scene, looking back at his sour companions from the carriage with distaste. This is actually also in Sangster's script, though he imagined Harker looking back at the coach with "no resentment in his face." Obviously, either Terence Fisher or Van Eyssen disagreed.

Heeding the words of producer Tony Hinds to keep it cheap, Sangster describes the castle as "a cross between a house and a castle." In the film, Harker merely opens the door to the castle and walks inside, but Sangster planned on something a bit more foreboding. In his version, Harker must use a large knocker to pound on the door. When he does, a bat flutters in front of him for a good scare. From this point forward, until the entrance of the vampire bride, what plays out in the script and on the screen is the same. The dialogue between Harker and the bride is extended in the script. In the film, the bride's first words to Harker are, "You will help me, won't you?" In the text, her first lines are, "Will you tell him that you've seen me?"

"Who?" Harker responds.

"You mustn't tell him...promise me?" the woman pleads, still not naming Dracula.

Harker quizzically speaks his name, she nods, and he assures her that he won't. Then the dialogue that we see in the film begins.

Fisher decided to change Sangster's version of Dracula's entrance ever so slightly. After the

Valerie Gaunt as the vampire bride with John Van Eyssen as Jonathan Harker.
Horror of Dracula © 1957 Hammer Films

girl runs off, we hear Dracula off-screen call out to Harker. Fisher chooses to show Dracula first, standing atop the staircase, before he comes down and speaks. Actually, I only assumed it was Fisher who changed the scene, but in reality, it was Lee himself who altered it. Lee wrote on his copy of the script the following note: "Isn't it more effective to have presence bring J. round...no voice."[9]

Sangster's description of Dracula is also slightly different, as he has him wearing a cloak with a "high pointed collar" and also has him carrying a black hat. Sangster also suggested briefly showing Dracula's canines, though Fisher wisely saved that for later.

As to other differences, Sangster's version of Dracula is slightly more loquacious. But, the gist of the conversation is the same, with Harker stating his enthusiasm to begin work and Dracula acting as though he's happy to have him there. Notably, in Sangster's script, Dracula says, "...it is most

unfortunate that I have to go again immediately. Your impressions of me as a host must be abysmal..."

Also, in the script, on the way to Harker's room, Harker takes note of a door in the hallway slowly closing shut, implying that the woman has been watching him again. No such scene or hint of it occurs in the film.

The dialogue between Harker and Dracula is somewhat rearranged from the script in the movie. On film, Dracula informs Harker that he must go out on business and won't be back until sundown tomorrow. He leaves the room, and Harker takes out a photo of Lucy Holmwood and places it on his desk. Dracula then walks back into the room to give Harker a key to the library and notices the photograph. In the script, a nosy Dracula spots the picture within Harker's suitcase and asks if he may take it out and look at it! After having examined the photo, he leaves the room and doesn't return.

Fisher again improves upon the structure of Sangster's script when

Harker goes to write in his diary. In the script, Harker observes Dracula leaving the castle, "his billowing cloak [creating] the impression of a giant bat flying..." After observing this, Harker goes to write in his diary, and we were to fade out on an image of the diary page. Fisher's transition is more dynamic, as Harker goes to write in his diary first, and we cut to Dracula (accompanied by his wonderful theme) walking into the night for the end of the scene.

Having seen the film many times, I can safely say that Sangster's version of the following scene gives me a different perspective on the sequence between Harker and the bride. For starters, it had always been my assumption that this scene took place shortly before dawn on the cusp of the sunrise. Sangster makes it very clear that he wanted the scene to take place at night, describing Harker entering a room bathed in moonlight (I get no such impression from the film). The exchange between Harker and the woman is basically the same, but

with an added section of dialogue where the bride asks Harker, "You're not...not one of..."

Her sentence trails off, leaving me to wonder, is she asking Harker if he's a fellow vampire, or is she actually suspecting the truth, that he is a vampire hunter? In either case, Sangster's version of the scene gave me the impression that the bride is genuinely wanting to escape and begging for help. She only gives in to her base desires when she comes into close contact with Harker in his embrace. The film, on the other hand, gives me the impression that she is manipulating Harker into a false state of compassion. But that's just me.

Sangster's version of the scuffle with Dracula is slightly more violent. The only notable detail worth repeating is that Sangster envisioned Dracula with bloodstained clothes from his wild night out. Either the makeup men didn't want to go to the trouble to add this detail, or perhaps Hammer simply knew this might be too much for the censors. So too, did Sangster

Christopher Lee in his most famous role. Horror of Dracula © 1957 Hammer Films

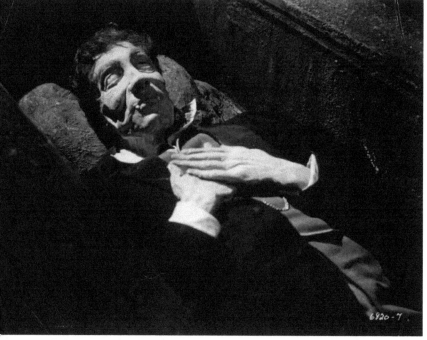

Deleted shot of the dummy built to resemble actor John Van Eyssen as Jonathan Harker. Horror of Dracula © 1957 Hammer Films

envision Harker finding the bride in her sarcophagus with blood dripping all the way down to her breasts (this was probably objected to by the censors). Fisher also chose not to show the staking itself (it's represented in shadow) so as to save it for Lucy's staking later.

Most film historians, like Ronald V. Borst, agree that Fisher's handling of Dracula's entrance into the scene is rather silly. As it is, Dracula leaves his coffin, goes outside, and comes back inside from the top of the staircase for dramatic effect. And it is dramatic for the audience, but within the world of the film it's a bit silly when one stops to think about it. Jimmy Sangster said that, "...the cut should have been to Dracula at the top of the steps just closing the door. In other words, he gone up the steps to close the door before coming back down."[10]

Sangster's idea, as written, was to have Dracula awaken. We would then get a POV shot of Dracula looking at Harker, who has his back turned, as the sun goes down. Dracula would then disappear and not be seen again. We were to simply hear the door atop the mausoleum close, followed by Harker's scream.

After the implied death of Harker, Van Helsing's introduction at the inn isn't terribly different in the script apart from a few details. The script has Van Helsing already in the inn, angrily questioning several men as to Harker's whereabouts to no avail, while Fisher chose to show Van Helsing enter the inn. Furthermore, the script sets up a subplot of sorts where the locals try their best at every turn to entice Van Helsing to leave. Though there are a few lines that imply this in the film, overall the subplot is watered down.

As we all know, Van Helsing eventually sets out for Dracula's castle to seek out Harker (unaware he is now a vampire). In the film, we see Harker, as played by Van Eyssen, sleeping in Dracula's old sarcophagus with vampire fangs. Not so in Sangster's script, where he describes Harker as looking like he has been drained of all blood and is a "living skeleton" with a malevolent smile. To film Sangster's version of the scene, a dummy was created. Photographs were taken of it, but it's unknown if any scenes were shot with it. Fisher apparently felt it more effective to simply have Van Eyssen for the shot. Furthermore, as Van Helsing prepares to stake Harker, Sangster imagined looping in a V.O. from Harker's diary: "I can only pray that whoever discovers my body will have the knowledge to do what is necessary to release my soul."

Moving onto the script's second act, Sangster's version of Arthur Holmwood is a bit of a hothead, and many of his angrier lines were deleted by the time of shooting. For instance, when Van Helsing informs Arthur that Harker was cremated on his authority, Arthur exclaims, "You're out of your mind...you're insane." Furthermore, after Van Helsing leaves (he is not escorted out by Gerta in the script) Arthur says, "I shall report his actions to the police."

The Holmwood's visit with Lucy also has some enlightening dialogue cut from the film that reveals that Arthur and Mina are themselves newlyweds. Lucy says to them, "Now why don't the two of you go

Peter Cushing as Professor Van Helsing.
Horror of Dracula © 1957 Hammer Films

into the parlour and turn down the lights...or has the novelty worn off after only a month of wedded bliss."

Sangster's version and Fisher's version of the scene where Lucy prepares for Dracula's arrival are similar, but Sangster envisioned showing the bite marks on Lucy's neck as soon as the Holmwoods left her room. Fisher wisely let this be the scene's final big reveal before cutting to Van Helsing.

What Van Helsing's Dictaphone reads back to him in the following scene was changed from the script. In the text, it reads like a P.I.'s monologue discussing a murder case, as Van Helsing ruminates over past events regarding Harker's death. But, in the film, it enlightens we, the audience, as to "seven facts" regarding vampirism. The purpose of the inn worker who comes into his room also differs. In the film, he comes because Van Helsing has called him to fetch a letter. In the script, the worker is pressuring Van Helsing as to how long he plans to stay at the inn—carrying over the theme of the townspeople wanting Van Helsing to leave.

Also, in the script, Van Helsing's final line spoken into his Dictaphone is a muse, wondering what Dracula wanted with the photo of Lucy. The film ends the scene with him stating that the vampire king must be destroyed, at which point we cut to Dracula standing outside Lucy's open window in both versions.

The following scene has Mina Holmwood walking out of Lucy's room with a doctor who has just examined her. As it turns out, this is Dr. Seward, one of the main characters in Stoker's novel, relegated to a cameo in this iteration. Sangster says that three of his scenes (numbers 48-50 to be exact) involving Dr. Seward examining Lucy were cut. Sangster speculated that they were probably taken out for the sake of the run time, and wrote that, "...I doubt [they were shot], because in subsequent scenes, the doctor is just a rather ineffectual character and no longer the pompous arsehole as I wrote him."[11]

As to what he means by Seward being a "pompous arsehole," this is likely due to the belittling attitude he has towards Gerta. When Mina tells him how worried Gerta is, Seward says that a "domestics place is in the kitchen." He's also a tad patronizing to Mina as he examines Lucy. Speaking of the examination scene, it was probably cut because it was too similar to the scene of Van Helsing later examining Lucy when she dies.

The meeting scene where Mina goes to see Van Helsing is also softened a bit. In the script, it is he who demands to see Lucy when he learns she is sick. He exclaims, "This time your husband will not stop me." In the film, it is Mina who invites Van Helsing to examine Lucy as a second opinion.

Our next deleted scene has Mina placing the garlic flowers in Lucy's room. When Lucy remarks upon the terrible smell, Mina says, "That's probably why [Van Helsing] suggested them. You've been bitten by something...the garlic is to keep it out of the room." If only she knew. Before Mina leaves, we also learn she and Arthur are going out on a business dinner. Also deleted, or left un-shot, was a scene of Gerta bidding the Holmwoods goodbye as they leave.

The scene where Lucy is found dead the next morning is tenser, with Van Helsing being confronted by Seward and Arthur when he appears. It's also interesting to note that Seward mentions how he's heard of Van Helsing before and knows that he's an "important man" as he puts it. The script's version of this scene ends with Van Helsing angrily informing everyone there that had they followed his instructions Lucy would still be alive. The film ends with Van Helsing giving Arthur the diary of Jonathon to read for himself.

As it turns out, Fisher more or less combined the scene in the film with a deleted scene from the script (which was most certainly not shot). The following scene in the script is Lucy's funeral, likely cut as an expense. Since the tomb set was already built as it appears later in the film, the added expense would have been in the form of the actors needed to play the priest and selected mourners. The scene has a procession led into the family tomb, and afterward Van Helsing approaches Arthur to give him Jonathan's diary.

The following sequence, where a policeman brings Tanya (Gerda's little girl) home to the Holmwoods, is also extended in Sangster's script. Here, Tanya is named Vera, and after Tanya/Vera's reveal that she saw Lucy, the policeman tries to question Holmwood about her. In the film, we fade into the graveyard shortly after Lucy's name has been dropped. In the script, the policeman would seem to imply that Lucy was trying to entice Vera into a "nasty business." When he insists on questioning Lucy, Arthur informs him that she died three days ago and we fade to the cemetery.

This is followed by another trivial deleted scene that would have shown Gerda sleeping. Next to her is an empty cot meant to imply Vera's absence. We would then cut

Van Helsing confronts Lucy.
Horror of Dracula © 1957 Hammer Films

to Vera out wandering in the night. After she regroups with Lucy and the duo walk to the crypt, there is a very telling line that was cut. Vera says, "Aunt Lucy, my neck is sore." Lucy then offers to kiss it again to make it better. Clearly, in Sangster's script, the child has already been bitten, but no implication is made in the film that she was. To hit the point home, Sangster wanted blood to be visible on Lucy's chin.

While many of Sangster's scenes are long on dialogue, his scene for the staking of Lucy is incredibly short. Van Helsing says nothing to Arthur as he approaches Lucy's tomb with a hammer and a stake. Arthur says, "I will do it…It is my responsibility…and it is my fault that it happened." This is the only dialogue in the scene before he goes to stake her!

In the film, Van Helsing explains what must be done. Furthermore, Van Helsing suggests they use Lucy to lead them to Dracula, which Arthur refuses. Arthur leaves the

tomb to take Tanya home and return at sunrise, while in the script Arthur stakes his sister then and there. In the film, Van Helsing does the deed (though, in the script, Arthur begins the process but can't seem to finish it so Van Helsing does).

The next scene takes place in Van Helsing's room at the inn with Arthur. Sangster's version has a slightly different tone, with Van Helsing still lamenting the loss of Lucy as his only lead to Dracula. As Van Helsing attempts to teach Arthur the ways to defeat the vampires, Arthur asks why then couldn't they have simply exposed Lucy to sunlight instead of traumatically driving a stake through her heart. It is here that Sangster reveals yet another twist on the mythos. Van Helsing claims that only a stake through the heart releases the soul back to purity, while death by the sunlight will not! Since Dracula was to perish by sunlight, perhaps Sangster wanted

Excellent publicity still of Christopher Lee and Melissa Stribling.
Horror of Dracula © 1957 Hammer Films

us to know that his soul would regain no sense of purity.

More differences follow. When Van Helsing goes to see the customs official about the whereabouts of the hearse and the coffin, in the film, this is intercut with Mina's scene. In the script, Mina's scene comes first and isn't intercut with the customs office scene. Furthermore, Van Helsing gets the information he seeks by yelling at the man in the script, but the movie gets a laugh when Arthur simply bribes him—the movie's version is better.

The scene of Arthur and Van Helsing trying their best to track Dracula's missing coffin, set in the Holmwood parlor where Mina sits knitting, is greatly condensed in the film. The script is wrought with exposition, such as Van Helsing mentioning a honeycomb of tunnels that Dracula can hide within beneath his castle. A seemingly skeptical Mina (by now bitten by Dracula) questions the men on their superstitions. Van Helsing shares with her a story about a cursed village in Transylvania that would allow within it no holy symbols of

the church. Van Helsing relates how the villagers searched him and took from him a small crucifix. He takes it from his pocket and then tosses it Mina. When she catches it, it burns her hand.

In the film, this is all simplified by having Arthur ask Mina to carry the cross for protection. Things play out similarly in both versions for a bit, though Sangster envisioned more blood on Mina in the aftermath of Dracula's attack. The discovery of Dracula's coffin in the cellar is handled differently in terms of the dialogue leading up to it (Gerda asks about a strange box in the cellar rather than refusing to go down there), but otherwise is like the film's version. Sangster also gives the frantic Gerda an extra line about how Dracula looked like a giant bat due to his fluttering cape that was cut.

Though the movie doesn't bother to tell us how Dracula acquired his getaway coach, the script does. In the scene, a coach driver whistles to himself along a lonely road when he spots a woman lying unconscious in his way. It is Mina. He dismounts the carriage to check on her. The scene would have ended with the coach driver looking behind him to see Dracula standing over him. From there, we would have dissolved into the following scene, where Van Helsing finds the dead man's body. This scene is in the film too, but in the script, Van Helsing states that the man's throat has been cut (if this is to imply that Dracula bit his throat or to suggest that he literally "cut his throat" is unknown).

Usually, Sangster's cut dialogue was no loss, but the script has some exposition between Van Helsing and Arthur that I found illuminating. As a kid, I had always wondered why on Earth Dracula was burying Mina in the ground. In fact, I found the scene almost comical (probably because, in my mind, I can't imagine Dracula using a shovel). Sangster offers an explanation via Van Helsing though.

The good doctor informs Arthur that Dracula will bury Mina in the ground. "If she dies while enclosed in Dracula's native soil, she will rise again when he chooses to call." Actually, the rules of vampirism aren't terribly well explained in the film, but several times in the script Sangster makes it clear that a woman bitten by Dracula must actually die before she becomes a vampire herself. Therefore, it's a bit clearer that by killing Dracula, Mina will never become a vampire herself.

In the film, we will also remember a humorous scene where Dracula's coach crashes through a border checkpoint, and upon being repaired, Van Helsing bursts through it next. In the script, Van Helsing actually stops to speak to the official. The official informs him that he must fill out the proper paperwork first. As he walks inside, he hears another crash and Van Helsing does what Dracula did earlier. Once again, the film's version is better. Following this, there was also supposed to be another humorous scene where the villagers watch Dracula's coach race by followed by Van Helsing's that was never shot.

As all Hammer aficionados will already know, the original climax was a bit less exciting. As soon as Dracula slams shut the trap door, Van Helsing busts out his crucifix and forces Dracula into the sunlight. That's basically it. To his credit though, Sangster's disintegration scene as written is close to what occurred in the film's uncut version—we'll get onto that in a moment.

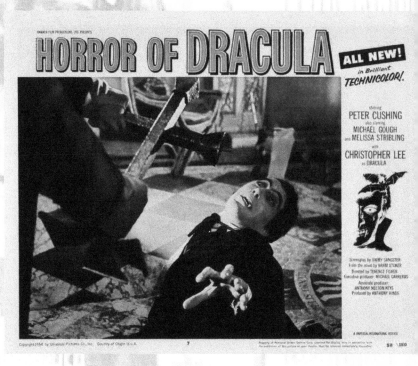

Excellent stills of the disintegration scene. Horror of Dracula © 1957 Hammer Films

Peter Cushing felt Van Helsing's finishing move on Dracula as it was lacked excitement. In *Flesh and Blood: The Hammer Heritage of Horror*, he joked that he had brandished so many crosses already throughout the film that he felt a bit like a crucifix traveling salesman! He felt that to bust out another was too easy, and so suggested that Van Helsing make one out of candlesticks. Allegedly, this idea came from the 1933 film *Berkeley Square*, starring Leslie Howard. It was also Cushing's idea to run across the table and tear down the curtains.

Though Cushing and Fisher changed his ending, Sangster maintains that it's actually his favorite scene in the film! "Shows I'm very amendable. My choice as best scene and I didn't even write it."[12]

To finish discussing Sangster's script, he envisioned the final shot taking place outside as Van Helsing reunites with Mina and Arthur. Birds were to begin singing, tying into the opening where Harker remarks that no birds were singing outside the castle. It's unknown if this scene was shot, and the film rolls the credits over Dracula's signet ring.

Now, onto the disintegration scene. For years fans talked about a "lost" Japanese cut of the film, which included an even more grotesque, extended version of the scene. Though men like Michael Carreras had more or less confirmed that extra footage was shot for Japan (where censors were less strict) in

Towa
HORROR OF DRACULA
colour by TECHNICOLOR
人間の生血に飢えて深夜の墓地を
さまよう戦慄の悪魔！
色彩も生々しき空前の猟奇巨篇！
鬼才 テレンス・フィッシャー監督
ピーター・カッシング
クリストファー・リー
吸血鬼ドラキュラ

PETER CUSHING
in
"DRACULA"
IN EASTMAN COLOUR   X
Also starring
MICHAEL GOUGH and MELISSA STRIBLING
with
CHRISTOPHER LEE
as DRACULA
A UNIVERSAL-INTERNATIONAL PRESENTATION
OF A HAMMER FILM PRODUCTION
RANK FILM DISTRIBUTORS LTD.

interviews, said footage could never quite be found.[13]

Then, in 2010, a writer/cartoonist named Simon Rowson, who lived in Japan, got to digging. A friend, Stuart Hall, had suggested that Rowson look for the lost footage via a post in the British Horror Forum. Rowson's wife Michiko suggested that he look for it in the archive of the National Film Center outside Tokyo. At first, things looked bleak. As it turned out, the Center's print of *Dracula* had been partially destroyed in a 1984 fire. Luckily, this comprised of the first five reels, which had no additional footage anyways. Fortunately, reels 6, 7, 8, and 9 survived the fire.

Eventually, Rowson was able to view the footage and confirmed that it was indeed an extended cut. And it wasn't just relative to the ending. The first extended scene concerned Dracula's assault of Mina in her home. It's a bit more suggestive and shows Dracula push her onto the bed. Actually, it's not just an extended scene, but it also utilized a different camera angle that shows Dracula's gaping mouth as he moves in to bite Mina.

The disintegration scene had extended shots of Dracula's legs and arms beginning to turn to dust. In the normal version, we see his leg begin to deflate, so to speak, but in the extended version his pant leg begins to roll up exposing his charred flesh. The same is true of the shot of his hand. The real gem of the bunch shows Christopher Lee in grotesque makeup, clawing the skin off of his face as he utters a terrible groan! There's also a short shot Van Helsing reacting to this in disgust.[14]

Rowson was ecstatic to report his find to the BFI, but before he could a horrible earthquake struck Japan only two days later. Once again, the film reels were in danger of becoming lost. But, just as they survived the fire, they also survived the earthquake. In 2012 began a process on the part of the BFI to restore the film to its full, uncut version, which is today available on Blu-Ray in Great Britain.

[1] They did still play in re-releases and eventually on television, where they were popular.

[2] The original *Curse of Frankenstein* was envisioned as being in black and white and starring Boris Karloff as Baron Frankenstein! Six-foot, five-inch comedic actor Bernard Bresslaw was considered for the role of the creature.

[3] Sangster specifically created a Reinfield-like character for *Dracula, Prince of Darkness* (1965) because of this, though.

[4] I will say that Sangster misspells Van Helsing as "Van Hesling" throught the entire script, but I will not repeat that spelling error in the main text.

[5] Coincidence or not, a fat worried merchant in a stage coach figures heavily into the opening scenes of *Taste the Blood of Dracula* (1970).

[6] Borst, "Production Background", *The Horror of Dracula*, pp.17.

[7] Fellner, *Encyclopedia of Hammer*, pp.112.

[8] Sangster, *Inside Hammer*, pp.46.

[9] Borst, "Production Background", *The Horror of Dracula*, pp.18.

[10] Ibid, pp.21.

[11] Ibid, pp. 47.

[12] Ibid, pp.49.

[13] They began this trend on *Curse of Frankenstein*.

[14] In the 1970s, the famed Toho Studios of Japan, which created Godzilla, did their own take on Hammer's vampire films with *Lake of Dracula* (1971). That film's ending is an homage to both *Dracula Has Risen from the Grave* (1968) and *Dracula*. In fact, the vampire's end disintegration is a near shot for shot remake of the uncut Japanese version of *Dracula* from 1958.

CARNOSAURs

That Could Have Been...

by Joey Palinkas

Remember your local video stores where you could rent a VHS? The joy of wandering in, catching the latest thrill in the horror section? Since my first experience with *Carnosaur*, I've never seen dinosaurs the same. I popped it in the VCR, spending the night in chills, my twelve year old self in awe of the film.

By this point I was a huge fan of classic monsters such as Godzilla, Gorgo, Rodan, Ray Harryhausen films, you name it! I also loved *Jurassic Park*. Yet, *Jurassic Park* was the glowing golden child that overshadowed *Carnosaur*, the novel and the film...

On that note, it wasn't until 2012 that I found out that *Carnosaur* was based off a novel. I went ahead and picked up a rather pricy copy. I spent a whole day reading it, taking my time with it. John Bronsnan (alias Harry Adam Knight) was an Australian author who had a fun writing style, consisting of three elements that I noticed: dark humor, carnage and sex. All three didn't hold back, and *Carnosaur* was the most extreme out of all his efforts. And whereas I liked the film, I loved the novel.

However, the film adaptation is only loosely based off the novel—and it's an adaptation by low budget movie king Roger Corman at that. Sadly, because of budgetary reasons, the film couldn't quite live up to the novel.

1984 CARNOSAUR

The 1984 novel *Carnosaur* is about a mysterious creature that goes on a rampant murder spree. (In the *Jurassic Park* novel, it's a series of strange animal attacks occurring in Costa Rica). The creature is believed to be a Siberian tiger that has escaped from a private zoo owned by Lord Darren Penward, the villain of the story. Reporter David Pascal investigates all the carnage and each time notices the scene of the crime has always been thoroughly cleansed. The creature's final attack takes place at a horse stable, killing a horse, the keep, and her daughter, though an eight year old boy survives.

Pascal arrives in time to see Penward's men towing away a concealed animal in a helicopter. Pascal interviews the boy, who reveals that is was a dinosaur. Pascal then tries to interview

Penward's men but is unsuccessful. Pascal then meets up with Penward's wife, simply referred as "Lady Penward" who is a bar fly/nymphomaniac.

David exploits the situation, beginning a relationship so he can get on the inside. After being taken to her private quarters, Pascal explores the estate and discovers a zoo comprising of a variety of modern wild animals and dinosaurs. He is captured by Penward and his men and is given a tour of the zoo, showing off many different kinds of species: a Scolosaurus, a Dilophosaurus, a Plesiosaurus, a Tarbosaurus, a Megalosaurus, an Altispinax-like dinosaur, possibly a Spinosaurus or Baryonx, and a Deinonychus (which was the creature that had escaped earlier).

Penward explains he recreated the creatures by studying DNA fragments found in dinosaur fossils, using them as a basis for restructuring the DNA of chickens. (Almost similar to Michael Crichton's *Jurassic Park* BUT those dinosaurs were recreated using damaged dinosaur DNA found in gnats, ticks, and mosquitoes fossilized in amber. Also gaps in the genetic codes were filled in with reptilian, avian, or amphibian DNA). Penward intends to let the creatures loose in remote areas of the world where they can flourish after an inevitable Third World War occurs (a common theme in Brosnan's novels).

Pascal is imprisoned, but is rescued by Lady Penward. As they make their escape, Pascal notices that his ex-girlfriend, Jenny Stamper (also a reporter), has been caught infiltrating the zoo as well. Lady Penward, enraged by jealousy, releases the dinosaurs and other

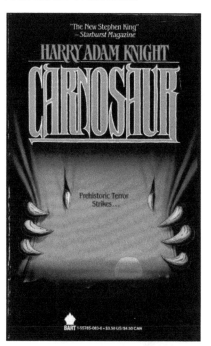

The *Carnosaur* novel.

animals. (In *Jurassic World: Fallen Kingdom*, dinosaurs are released from their holding pens under the Lockwood estate, similar to this novel's third act).

In the chaos, the Tarbosaurus destroys Penward's helicopter before he can enter it. The Deinoychus pursues Pascal and Jenny through Penward's museum. This is similar to the scene in *Jurassic Park* where the raptors follow Lex and Tim Murphy into the kitchen. It's also similar to *Jurassic World: Fallen Kingdom*, when the Indoraptor chases the cast through the museum.

While being chased through the estate they stumble upon a guard with one arm torn off, reaching out for help. (Coincidentally, *Jurassic World: Fallen Kingdom* was supposed to have a scene where the Indoraptor kills a guard in the same fashion. Also, the character of Iris is confronted by the Indoraptor, resulting in a similar fate).

They trick the Deinoychus into attacking its own reflection and escape (in *Jurassic Park*, note Lex's move to trick the raptor in the kitchen). The other dinosaurs go on a rampage downtown and most of them are killed by the British Army—but not until after the town is in complete chaos. (This is one of the biggest scenes of carnage, and is quite insane). The Tarbosaurus is the final big dinosaur of the story as it's fought off by firetrucks with high pressure water and a support pillar causes its death.

The next morning, Pascal goes home to visit Jenny, only to find her alive but missing an arm and her family dead by the Deinoychus. Pascal kills it with a pitchfork. They live and get back together. Meanwhile Lord Penward is held up in a farmhouse and has tied up his wife. He then unleashes two baby Tyrannosaurus so that she is devoured alive.

Don't Trust The Cake

Brosnan stated he became interested in writing a novel about dinosaurs after a colleague of his returned from Hollywood. The friend indicated that a fad of dinosaur fever might occur within the next decade. Brosnan published his book in 1984 via Star Books, and like most of his work, received little attention in the U.K. In 1989 it was published in the U.S. by Bart Books, which had a small following in Texas.

In 1991, Roger Corman's wife, Julie contacted Brosnan for the film rights for a film adaptation. Corman secured the rights for the film and began production as soon as he learned *Jurassic Park* had been greenlit. A very interesting fanzine article by John Brosnan, explains a

lot of what went wrong with the film.

Brosnan began his reminiscence in mid-1991, when an American woman rang him on the phone one morning and asked if he was Harry Adam Knight. Suspicious, Brosnan told her that he 'sort' of was. The woman turned out to be Julie Corman, wife of B-movie King Roger Corman. Not only did Roger want to buy the film rights to *Carnosaur*, he also wanted Brosnan to write the screenplay. Brosnan at first thought that it might be a practical joke but was thrilled to find she was serious. Brosnan met Julie Corman at his favorite bar that night and she drew up the contract on a couple of the club's paper napkins! "[It was] just like Godard and Cannon once did at Cannes. Gosh! A dream come true! I would be getting a screenwriting credit on a Hollywood movie! Hah!" Brosnan recollected.

Brosnan then went on to explain how *Carnosaur* came to be to begin with. He remembered that back in 1983, a film journalist colleague of his, Alan Jones, had just returned from a visit to Hollywood. According to Jones, the next big Hollywood trend would be dinosaur movies. "A whole, big line-up of dino pics were on the drawing boards, he told me. So I immediately came up with a clever and cunning plan. I quickly whipped up an outline about genetically engineered dinosaurs being created in a private zoo owned by a deranged aristocrat in deepest Cambridgeshire," Brosnan said.

Naturally, the dinosaurs escape the private zoo and cause all sorts of carnage. Brosnan sent the story to the editor at Star who had bought *Slimer* [a 1983 horror novel by Brosnan], and it was published in 1984. Unfortunately, the prophesied dino-movie craze never took off. In fact, one of the only ones to be produced was *Baby: Secret of the Lost Legend*. "But as hack novels go I thought, and still do, that *Carnosaur* was pretty good and I also thought, at the time, that it might do well. It didn't," Brosnan remembered.

Like *Slimer*, Carnosaur "sank without a trace." The book received a limited distribution in the States. A friend of Brosnan's, Lisa Tuttle, told him that in her hometown of Austin, Texas, that *Carnosaur* had developed "a small, hard-core group of fans" in 1987. By 1989, Carnosaur was published in the U.S. again by a small paperback company called Bart Books. Unfortunately, the publisher went under soon after. Around that time Brosnan heard about Steven Spielberg's plan to make a dinosaur movie called *Jurassic Park* based on Michael Crichton's book. "The film got postponed but Crichton's novel turned up in 1991," Brosnan wrote.

Naturally, Brosnan was curious about the similarities to his novel and bought a copy of the book. Intrigued by reviews that lauded the book, Brosnan "noticed a lot of interesting similarities (e.g., the same dinosaurs were described in the same 'unique' way) between it and Carnosaur." Brosnan was pondering what to about the situation when the call from Corman came.

Brosnan admits that he was suspicious about being offered the chance to write the screenplay. Brosnan was smart enough to guess that it was a ploy to sweeten Corman's financial offer which, which was already pretty small by Hollywood standards.

Brosnan recalled,

Anyway, I first wrote an outline, as requested, and sent it off to Corman who was staying in Paris. He rang me a couple of times on a pay phone which kept cutting him off in mid-sentence. An inauspicious start to our relationship I thought. When he finally got to a phone that worked he made a few useful suggestions about the plot before he dropped a bombshell.

I'd assumed, seeing as he was trying to compete with *Jurassic Park*, that he would be making Carnosaur on a bigger budget than he spent on the usual Corman product. But no, he told me the budget would be one million dollars. I couldn't see how Carnosaur could be made for that amount of money so I asked if I should drastically cut back on the dinosaur scenes in the first draft. He said, no, I was to write whatever I wanted and that modifications would be made in the later drafts. Hmm. So I wrote the first draft, sent it to him in Hollywood, and never heard another word from him. The shutters came down - clank! - and all lines of communication were cut.

Corman had what he wanted - by that time the official contract for the rights had been signed and sealed - and I was no longer needed. One of his minions did eventually write - after many faxes from my agent - to say that my screenplay was okay considering I'd never written one before (I'd written several) but that Corman would be using writers more familiar with his working methods. Ho ho. Time passed, as it tends to do, and I heard various rumours about the making of Carnosaur; ie, that all the dinosaurs had been reduced to one (actually two,

Roger Corman on *Entertainment Tonight*.

Tyrannosaurus and Deinonychus) and that it was being achieved with a glove puppet.[1]

However, Brosnan received a ray of hope from Alan Jones, back from another trip to Hollywood. Jones said that he visited the *Carnosaur* set and that he was highly impressed by the dinosaur models. After this, *Carnosaur* got previewed in the U.S. and supposedly received good reviews.

Brosnan concluded his piece writing,

My hopes rose further. Then bloody Alan Jones returned from a film festival in Milan where *Carnosaur* was screened and said, "It's crap."

I've since seen it on video and yes, it is crap and, compared to the film of *Jurassic Park* the dinosaurs are laughable, but it's interesting crap. And thanks to the movie the novel has been reprinted both in the States and here in the U.K. And in fact we are having a re-launch party of the book at my drinking club this very night. The video will also be screened and I will no

doubt take the lead in shouting abuse at the screen.

1993 CARNOSAUR

According to co-producer Mike Elliot, Corman "felt that now was the time to shoot our movie, because he knew he could make the movie faster than anybody else and get it out of there first".[2]

The 1993 *Carnosaur* film, opens up to an unintentionally hilarious scene set within a chicken plant, foreshadowing the creation of the carnosaurs. Dr. Jane Tiptree (Diane Ladd), instead of sir Penward, has been in quiet research for the Eunice Corporation. DARPA is concerned about her work with genetically modified chickens but legally cannot interfere in her research for three years.

While transporting Tiptree's chickens from the poultry farm,[3] one of the eggs hatches and a baby Deinonychus kills the driver and escapes. Meanwhile, in a small Nevada town (instead of Cambridgeshire England), the populace begins suffering a mysterious flu like illness.

Nearby at a Eunice owned quarry, Doc Smith (the stand in for David Pascal), a watchman protecting excavation equipment from environmentalists, meets Ann Thrush (the stand in for Jenny Stamper). Meanwhile there are a series of gruesome killings, assumed to be a bobcat instead of a Siberian tiger. Among the victims is the daughter of Eunice employee Jesse Paloma. He threatens to take his story to the press, but Tiptree tricks and lures him into a laser protected pen where a fully grown Tyrannosaur eats him.

In spite of the murders, Thrush and a group of the environmentalists handcuff themselves to the excavation equipment to protest. Everyone except Thrush is torn to shreds and killed by the Deinonychus. Thrush is then rescued by Doc but is attacked again and fires a rifle shell at the Deinonychus who is frightened away.

Doc then discovers a Eunice truck with two dead men inside, disemboweled. Deducting the creature originated from the facility, he contacts Tiptree announcing he caught the animal and has hidden the body.

Meanwhile the town sheriff is making eggs and discovers a dinosaur embryo within one of them and takes it to a doctor for investigation. Elsewhere, Doc infiltrates the laboratory, Tiptree checks the bodybag discovering her flaw, and Doc corners her at gunpoint. She then reveals her experiments to him. The mysterious flu illness is caused by infected chicken eggs containing a lethal airborne virus that also impregnates women with dinosaur embryos. Similar to the novel's extremist POV regarding dinosaurs inheriting the Earth after a third world war, Ladd gives a chilling performance as her character explains that this is her way of exterminating the human race and replacing it with dinosaurs. The government and DARPA trace the towns deaths back to Eunice, and place the entire town under quarantine. The military men are

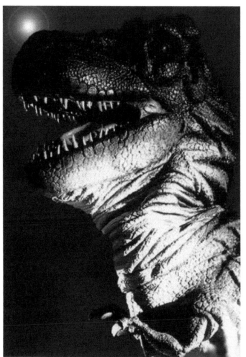

Carnosaur's T-Rex. © 1993 New Horizons Pictures

told to kill all civilians on sight, infected or not.

The town sheriff responds to a disturbance call at the local kennel. He finds the Deinonychus, which he incapacitates with a shotgun blast to the chest. Foolishly, as he inspects the beast, it jabs its toe claw through his stomach. Aiming the shotgun at the creature's face, he blasts it away for good. Elsewhere, Government officials begin plotting the repopulation of the human race in response to the virus including a new social order with strict fertilization policies and artificial wombs.

Doc obtains the anti-virus and makes an escape. But, the Tyrannosaurus is let loose by Tiptree and chases after Doc out of the facility. Tiptree births a dinosaur as it tears through her stomach a la *Alien*. Doc returns to

the quarry, followed by the T-Rex, only to learn Thrush is gravely ill. Doc dispatches the T-Rex with a backhoe loader, and then rushes to give Thrush a dose of the anti-virus. In a downer of an ending, government hazmats arrive to gun down the duo and burn their bodies!

Interesting "Crap"

The new story, loosely based off Brosnan's novel, was an interesting concept and well executed for the budget given. It's amazing to ponder at what this film could have been with a bigger budget and a better production company not just looking to make their next popcorn flick, which at best, is what the film is.

The novel had an impressive line of dinosaurs featured. More dinosaurs were included in

Brosnan's first draft, but sadly after Corman cut ties with the author, the number of dinosaurs were reduced and we were left with a very impressive animatronic Tyrannosaurs and a gawky Deinoychus.

Tony Doublin, stated that "they shot special effects within three days".[2] Working with the likes of the now late John Carl Buechler and his company Magical Media Industries, the crew spent ten weeks constructing a full scale 16ft Tyrannosaurs, plus a smaller scale Tyrannosaur that didn't quite resemble the animatronic, (featured on the box art). Lastly, there was a puppet and a suit for the Deinoychus.

Adam Simon was hired as director, but, according to Doublin, "the director was nowhere to be found, they were alone to do their work." Ultimately, the producers set out to make a low budget horror film, estimated at $1 million dollars, but in reality only used $850,000 for the film.

On May 14, 1993, *Carnosaur* opened in the U.S. and grossed $1.8 million in total despite Corman being optimistic that people who were going to see *Jurassic Park* that June would also see *Carnosaur*. Word on the novel eventually spilled out resulting in a small print run of Brosnan's novel in the states in 1994. And, despite the less than stellar grosses, the film developed a cult following. Therefore the sequel, *Carnosaur 2* was rushed into production, with Louis Morneau in the director's chair.

CARNOSAURS

Carnosaur 2 was supposed to get a limited theatrical release (rumors say it actually did) but ultimately was released direct to video in February of 1995. Interestingly

enough, *Carnosaur 2* was more entertaining than the original and scrapped the novel's ideas altogether. Essentially it was a mockbuster of *Aliens* only with dinosaurs.

The movie opens with a few random Yucca Mountain crew members being slaughtered. An electricity crew then gets called in for repairs at the facility, located 80 miles into the Nevada desert. Soon after they arrive they discover that the entire facility crew is missing. Only a lot of blood and a survivor, Jessie (the Newt stand in), are found. Searching the facility they discover that the Yucca mines are a repository for abandoned nuclear weapons from the Cold War, and that there are dinosaurs loose. (which essentially makes this like a film adaptation of Capcom's video game, *Dino Crisis*).

Jack Reed (the Ripley stand-in) demands answers from McQuade (the Burke stand-in), a government marshal, who at first pretends he knows nothing. But, after their chopper pilot is killed, he tells them the truth: that a brilliant genetic scientist (Tiptree) brought back the dinosaurs. (He doesn't elude to the horrid virus or the intentions of Dr. Tiptree, though). Jesse reveals he has access to dynamite and they plan to blow up the facility so the creatures don't escape.

McQuade is killed along with another tech named "Monk" (similar to the suicidal sacrifice in the tunnels in *Aliens*), which buys Jack and Jesse some time but Jack takes a long fall and is injured. Jesse runs outside and into the rescue team that was automatically called by the main computer crash distress call. He runs back inside to rescue Jack, from there they encounter the Tyrannosaur who chases them down an elevator (the

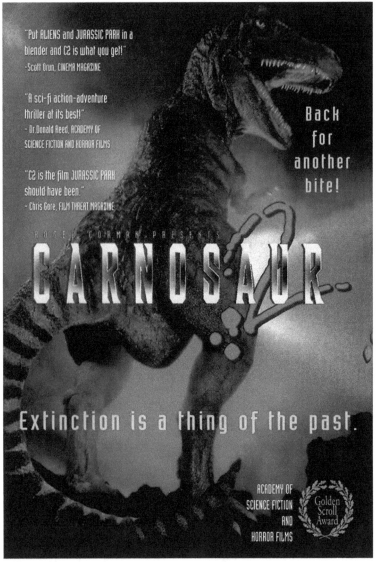

"Put ALIENS and JURASSIC PARK in a blender and C2 is what you get!"
-Scott Orun, CINEMA MAGAZINE

"A sci-fi action-adventure thriller at its best!"
- Dr.Donald Reed, ACADEMY OF SCIENCE FICTION AND HORROR FILMS

"C2 is the film JURASSIC PARK should have been."
- Chris Gore, FILM THREAT MAGAZINE

Back for another bite!

ROGER CORMAN PRESENTS

CARNOSAUR

Extinction is a thing of the past.

ACADEMY OF SCIENCE FICTION AND HORROR FILMS

Golden Scroll Award

beast literally climbs on top on the elevator and growls, resulting in one of the creepiest shots ever put on film)! They make it outside and Jesse battles the T-Rex via forklift (essentially recreating the ending of the first *Carnosaur* and *Aliens* all at once). Jesse pushes the creature down a long bay shaft which kills it upon impact. Jesse and Jack climb into the chopper and detonate the explosives... which somehow don't result in a meltdown.

This feature is considered the best of all the Carnosaur films and it's quite easy to see why. As already stated, it's just a retelling of *Aliens* but with dinosaurs—enough said!

The Tyrannosaurs animatronic was reused to save money. Yet, despite budget constraints, Magical Media Industries (now lead by Tony

Dublin and under observation by John Carl Buechler) added improvements to the T-Rex. Specifically they altered it so that it could be used more elaborately during the battle scene in which the dinosaur fights the forklift. However, the animatronic was still ill-suited for stunt work (such as the shots of the creature ramming the forklift), so miniatures and hand puppets were again used frequently, as in the first film.

Interestingly enough, the Deinoychus was replaced by Velociraptors, possibly due to the awareness and popularity of *Jurassic Park's* raptors. Magic Media Industries used the exact same Deinonychus costume molds to create the bodies for the Raptor costumes; only the heads and necks were changed to reflect the longer neck and snout that distinguish the two dinosaurs. Close-ups were achieved using puppet heads with mechanical devices.

It's also worth noting that by this point John Brosnan had withdrawn all involvement or associations with the *Carnosaur* sequels. It could even be argued that the popularity of *Carnosaur 2* even eclipsed interest in the novel.

Counter Strike Much?
The series continued down the direct to video route for the third and final film under the Carnosaur banner: *Carnosaur 3: Primal Species*. Jonathan Winfrey directed a script by Rob Kerchner and Constantine Nasr.

The third story revolves around an army convoy that is attacked by domestic terrorists who seem to be randomly attacking US convoy trucks that possibly contain uranium. Using a nearby dockside warehouse, they inspect the cargo and two frozen Velociraptors and a

Tyrannosaurs escape, killing all but one terrorist. Police arrive and hilariously leave the terrorist handcuffed and gagged in their squad car. More units arrive at the warehouse to deal with the assailants, who they assume are just drug smugglers. Opening a container, they are slaughtered by another raptor and the Tyrannosaurus, who was hiding behind the truck (yeah, no kidding).

A Counter Terrorist force led by Colonel Rance Higgins is called in to locate the missing containers. Upon arrival at the warehouse, two of them are killed. The survivors retreat and are informed by Dr. Hodges that these are the last three "carnosaurs" in existence, left from the genetic reconstructions of the previous Carnosaurs. In the interest of potentially curing major diseases, they must be captured.

A net trap is set up with meat (seems like a *Looney Tune* special, eh?). One of the raptors is seemingly shot and killed while attempting to grab a Counter Terrorist operative named "Polchek." They take the beast back to a makeshift tent for examination and somehow Dr. Hodges manages to deduct that the T-Rex is breeding (kinda like how the Kennys from the Gamera movies seem to somehow know this stuff). Hodges theorizes that Polchek's attempted abduction was to feed some new hatchlings (this is interesting since in the *Carnosaur* novel that the villain feeds his wife to T-Rex hatchling). The final plan is freeze the dinosaurs somehow, since the creatures are apparently cold blooded. The raptor then awakens and begins to attack. The T-Rex also appears and bites off a soldier's head before escaping with the Velociraptor.

When the time comes to explore the lower decks of the ship, the

carnosaurs knock out the lights and kill a couple more soldiers. The rest get to an elevator, but a raptor chews the cable through and they crash on the bottom level, discovering the nest of eggs which they begin to shoot, angering the T-Rex, who eats them.

The surviving marines and Dr. Hodges then rig up some C4. Then the T-Rex bursts through a ceiling and drags one of the marines through and kills him. The two Velociraptors attack, one rips off a marine's head and the other is shot to death before the other raptor is also shot.

Hodges senses the T-Rex is close, so she and Rance hide behind some lockers which the dinosaur head-butts. Rance throws C4 in its mouth, killing it. They then jump overboard to narrowly escape an explosion that decimates the whole ship.

The movie ends on a "button", or final gag. Remember that lone terrorist that was gagged and cuffed in the back seat of the police car? A random raptor appears and leers at him through the window. The man screams and we cut to the credits.

According to Tony Dublin, they reused all assets and miniatures for all three Carnosaur films. Due to the budget lowering with each entry, it was good use and money well spent. What they were able to accomplish on such a tight budget is incredible in hindsight.

Reboot Territory
It is believed that 2001's direct to video *Raptor* is an unofficial entry in the Carnosaur series. It was directed by exploitation creature feature extraordinaire Jim Wynorski, (*Piranhaconda*, etc.). However, *Raptor* almost seems to be more of a reboot of the entire series. It also takes more points from the novel. Yet, all that said, what it mostly does is recycle stock footage and assets from the three previous films. If you can discount the other entries, then this is a solid watch.

The film opens up with stock footage killings from *Carnosaur*. Sheriff Jim Tanner (the new stand-in for David Pascal) and his assistant Barbara (the Jenny Stamper stand-in) investigate a gruesome slaughter of three teens assuming it was a large cat like a cougar, (again, in the novel it was a Siberian tiger and in the 93' film it was a bobcat). Dr. Hyde (a stand in for Penward from the novel) gets debriefed by his henchmen (like in the novel) on the escape and recapture attempts of the Deinonychus, err, I mean Velociraptor. Just like in the 93' adaptation with Dr. Tiptree, he's a now former military researcher whose government funding for a dinosaur cloning project was cut.

Back to the sheriff, another murder occurs in the form of a truck driver stock footaged to death. This time the sheriff assumes it was a random slasher instead of a cougar. A deputy is slaughtered by the raptor soon after, then the film cuts to a sex scene with the Sherriff's daughter and her boyfriend. In the novel, there is a scene of a girl having sex with her boyfriend, who then is ripped out of the truck and killed. The girl flees in the truck and is killed by striking a tree, which snaps her neck. In *Raptor*, the boyfriend is killed and the sheriff's daughter takes off in the truck. Somehow the raptor is on the truck attacking her as she is driving and she decides to bail out. The vehicle then falls off the bridge and explodes.

Cutting to the aftermath of the chicken truck attack—where the driver was stock footaged to death earlier—Tanner assumes again that it was a cougar. Barbra notices how there are no tracks and that the crime scene appears to have been "cleaned up" similar, again, to the novel. Tanner discovers a truck log recording that the vehicle is registered to the Eunice company. Another deputy is called into town who faces off with the "raptor" but really it's just more stock footage of the sheriff from the first film, shotgunning the raptor. Barbara inspects the deputy's body and finds a large claw imbedded inside him.

At this point, you have to ask yourself why they didn't realize that it was a dinosaur that was killing everyone. Furthermore, according to the stock footage, the raptor's body should've been left behind for them to find too. But, it's assumed the body was recovered by Dr. Hyde's men. Tanner then calls around trying to locate any files on Eunice. In the scene, we see an FBI agent flipping open a dossier on Dr. Hyde, showing us what a hush up situation it really is.

The FBI agent then contacts the pentagon, who raises concerns about the twelve year project. An argument ensues about the termination of the project and it's mentioned that the fatalities around the vicinity of Hyde's research facility are similar to the "Jurassic Storm" project twelve years ago. Hyde denies the claims and seemingly the case is dropped.

Tanner investigates the facility with a search warrant with Barbra in tow. Together they get a tour of the facility. Down in the lower part of the facility, Hyde stops the tour at gunpoint. Tanner draws his firearm but Hyde's thugs are behind them, their weapons drawn (in the novel, Pascal is captured and escorted around in a similar way.)

One of the deputies contacts the FBI, whom is concerned by the fact that Tanner went missing over an hour ago upon investigation of the Facility. The FBI agent, again, contacts the pentagon general. He states that Hyde has lied to the government and has received foreign aid. A Special Ops team is sent in to shut down the project, and more stock footage entails.

Power is cut by the power company and the dinosaurs escape their pens. There is a Tyrannosaurus in the facility too, which escapes, (even though the film is called *Raptor*). Strategic use of stock footage from *Carnosaur 3* ensues, (honestly some of the best use of stock footage this author has ever seen). Ultimately, the plan is to blow up the facility.

Meanwhile, Dr. Hyde gives a speech to his handler, Karen. "For the greater good, we're scientists," he proclaims as the creatures are set loose. Dr. Hyde refuses to aid the Spec Ops team and instead lets them fall victim to the dinosaurs. (In the novel and the original film, the villain has a motive to restore the world with dinosaurs, while Hyde has a throwaway line along the lines of "imagine the world repopulated with the creatures!"). Tanner and the military escape the facility along with a ton of researchers. Hyde almost escapes dressed as a researcher, but is eaten by the Tyrannosaurus by way of *Carnosaur 2*.

The Special Ops starts unloading their weapons onto the stock footage T-Rex as Tanner jumps into a nearby Bobcat (cue more stock footage.) Barbara opens bay doors and Tanner uses the Bobcat to push the T-Rex into the pit. Shortly after the facility blows up via stock footage and the film ends. (Oh and there's a silly subplot about the human genome project and a cloned Dr. Hyde is revealed at an undisclosed facility!).[4]

You can see how *Raptor* is a more faithful adaption to Brosnan's novel than the '93 *Carnosaur* was, while also taking highlights from all three films. Essentially, it takes the best of both worlds, subtracting the virus subplot from the original film.

Verdict

Overall, the entire Carnosaur saga branched out into exploitative territory and ran with it. That being said, despite the '93 movie's subpar grosses, considering Corman managed to get two direct-to-video sequels out of it I guess he got his money's worth. Most retained what made the novel so good, such as the dark nature of dinosaurs, what we'd assume would happen if they came back, etc. As to how they were filmed, yes, most shots were quite dark as a means to hide flaws BUT, in those scenes, it really only amplified the atmosphere, making these creatures appear as if they were not supposed to be here naturally (in my opinion, at least).

Now, as for the million dollar question: What could the *Carnosaur* movie have been with a proper budget? What if Brosnan had held out for a company that could better produce his vision? What if it could have been more like 2017's adaptation of Stephen King's *It*? *It* did justice to the source material and resonated with audiences. In 2018, Concorde New Horizons, the company that produced these films, were sold by Roger Corman and his wife Julie to Shout Factory. The property *Carnosaur* at this time of writing, is lost and has fallen deeper into obscure hands. All films and the novel are out of print, and have been for a few years now. My personal hope is that one day the franchise will continue. After all, if *Jurassic Park* can get five sequels (dear lord, stop) then *Carnosaur* deserves a reboot!

---

[1] *You Only Live Once* (2007). https://efanzines.com/YOLO/YouOnlyLiveO nce.pdf.
[2] Ibid.
[3] Clint Howard's line "why such nervous chickens?" There is a hilarious riff of that comment from YouTube channel Brandon Tenold, check it out!) [https://youtube.com/watch?vViNJ2mfHwiw].
[4] Briefly I will mention "The Eden Formula" which was made for Television then released on DVD in 2007. Directed by *Carnosaurs* special effects director, John Carl Buechler. Once again using assets and a CGI Tyrannosaurs alongside a terrible reconstructed head (since it was blow apart in *Carnosaur 3*) to be the main villain of the film. It's about corporate spies breaking into a facility that is holding a Tyrannosaurs which escapes and kills some civilians and is lured to an IED and killed. Overall The Eden Formula, hardly has any connection to the Carnosaur series other than some assets and stock footage.

INTO THE CAVE
Debunking Myths of Kong's Spider Pit
by Kyle Byrd

Concept art for the mysterious "Spider Pit" scene by Mario Larrinaga.

One of the most famous pieces of lost film is without a doubt the deleted "spider pit" scene from 1933's *King Kong*. The sequence was to occur when a group of sailors try to run across a log above a ravine as the titular giant ape chases them through the jungle. In the film as we know it, Kong shakes the sailors off of the log as they fall into a cave and meet their demise. The scene was originally to last a bit longer as an assortment of oversized creepy crawlies (including a giant spider, a tentacled creature, a smaller trapdoor spider, a crab monster, and a giant lizard) would emerge in the cave and attack the sailors.

Over the years, there have been so many rumors about these missing seconds of footage that it is hard to keep track of them all. Some say the scene was in the first release of the film, but it was removed by censors for being too frightening. Others say they saw the scene themselves during later theatrical re-releases (this was even claimed by famous sci-fi author Ray Bradbury), although these statements are often dismissed as faulty memories. There is even debate as to whether or not the scene was actually filmed at all. All these rumors get repeated with varying nuances to this day. The truth is that the scene was cut for pacing reasons and only shown at a preview screening for RKO staff. *Kong* producer/co-director Merian C. Cooper confirmed this much and more in a letter to collector Jack Polito (as quoted in the book *Ray Harryhausen: Master of the Majicks*

Behind the scenes shot of the Spider Pit scene featuring the trapdoor spider and the giant crab in it. Used with permission from the collection of Willis and Darlyne O'Brien.

Vol: 1 by Mike Hankin). In the letter, Cooper stated, "The picture was running too long so I edited the original down. The spider sequence took the audiences' attention away from Kong; it stopped the flow of the action." Later in the letter he confirms the bleak fate of the footage. "All the scenes I removed were kept at RKO and were there when I left. RKO had a big fire in the 50s and much of their back lot and film library was destroyed. I believe the *Kong* material was part of what was lost. The spider sequence was never seen in any theater; I cut it out even before Steiner scored the picture." The publication of this letter puts most of the often-repeated rumors to rest. Except one.

For decades, rumors have persisted that *Kong* animator Willis "Obie" O'Brien reused the creature models from the spider-pit sequence for his work on the 1957

film *The Black Scorpion*, in which similar monsters appear in a sequence taking place in a cave (to this day, this is often repeated as a fact despite there being no actual evidence that confirms it). It is difficult to pinpoint where these rumors even originated. Thanks to images belonging to the late Darlyne O'Brien (Willis O'Brien's wife), we even have a good look at the creatures from *Kong* for comparison.

The script for *the Black Scorpion* was written to cash in on the success of giant bug films such as *Them!* (1954) and *Tarantula* (1955). When the project was offered to Willis O'Brien, he was desperate for work. His constant efforts to get new films off the ground were failures. He didn't want to resort to low budget b-films, but he reluctantly agreed, as he didn't have any other offers. Soon enough, he and fellow animator Pete Peterson would set up shop at the Tepeac Studio in Mexico City, working under a tiny budget and harsh working conditions. The low budget nature of *The Black Scorpion* only adds believability to the theory that models from *King Kong* were recycled.

For help in getting to the bottom of this, yours truly contacted prolific special effects artists Ernest Farino (*The Thing, Terminator*) and Mark Wolf (*Flight of the Navigator, The Age of Mammals*) to lend their encyclopedic knowledge of the subject. There are several repeated rumors around the usage of *Kong* models in *The Black Scorpion* but before those are examined, some obvious factors should be discussed. The most relevant issues would be the condition of the models themselves so much later and how *The Black Scorpion* (a Warner Bros. film) would have managed to use items belonging to another studio (*King Kong* was an RKO film). "It's general knowledge that Obie was just not someone who kept models or other memorabilia from his films. Plus, the *Kong* models would have been the property of RKO. . . .In this regard, the models would almost certainly be retained by RKO as their property. To re-use the models would have involved permission and licensing, possibly incurring a fee, all of which was not likely the case with a low budget independent production such as *The Black Scorpion*. In other words,

Three stills from *The Black Scorpion* featuring the worm monster.

more trouble than it's worth," Farino said. This means that the only way O'Brien and Peterson would have even gotten the models out of RKO would be if they snuck them out, which is not likely. It should also be mentioned that stop motion models degrade over time. Animator Jim Danforth described

45

***King Kong's* lost spider (above) and *The Black Scorpion's* spider creature (left).**

century after they were built. Therefore, it is highly unlikely that models that old would be in any kind of working condition.

Another factor that should be detailed is the changes in model construction in the years between *King Kong* and *The Black Scorpion,* as there had been advancements in the field. "For *Black Scorpion*, Obie embraced pioneering breakthroughs in model construction. In fact, this was the first use of new polyester resins, which were a good choice to simulate the appropriate chitinous look," said Mark Wolf. This is illustrated best by looking at how the tentacled worm creature (which has been rumored to be recycled from either the tentacled beast in the pit or the two-legged lizard we see attack Jack Driscoll in *Kong*) was constructed. The armature itself was a ball-joint construction, which would not have been used in the 1933 film. "The armature of the

his encounter with models from *King Kong* at RKO during the making of *Jack the Giant Killer* in his book *Dinosaurs, Dragons, and Drama*, which Farino cites. "Jim states in the chapter on *Jack the Giant Killer*, 'it had been decided that the armatures from *King Kong* were not suitable for modern animation.'" It wasn't just *Kong* models that were still in RKO storage either. Danforth also says he came across the Triceratops model from O'Brien's canceled *Gwangi* project. These tidbits confirm a few important details. This tells us that O'Brien didn't keep models from *Kong* (or other projects for that matter), but also that they were not fit for use a half-worm was entirely different from OBie's usual design and engineering, using ball and socket joints for the body segments, though the short tail was hinged. . . . Beyond the use of resins and totally different style of armature construction, the [lizard] puppet in *Kong* has a shape that is overall thinner and keeps reducing in dimensions all the way towards the tail. That is NOT the *Black Scorpion* worm which was uniformly bulky. . . . It is patently absurd to think the worm was re-used from *Kong*. Let's dispense with that as a false myth that is not worth perpetuating," Wolf clarified. (Wolf actually owned the worm puppet for several years).

This next brings us to the matter of *Kong's* spider critters, which are also often believed to have been reused. The large spider simply looks nothing like any of the monsters in *The Black Scorpion*, so that alone should be enough to shoot down any rumors of it being re-used. The issue of the smaller trapdoor spider is a bit greyer. Both films have trapdoor spider creatures that look extremely similar, as they both have only six legs (plus pedipalps) and a similar body type. In fact, a photo even exists of a surviving model being displayed publicly with a caption card describing it as a surviving *Kong* model! These facts make the rumors more believable, but they should not be an indicator that the creatures are one and the same. Furthermore, the fact that the two creatures look so similar could easily be due to the fact that O'Brien designed them both. A closer look at both creatures would show a different skin texture as well as leg shapes. Combined with the previously mentioned degradation of *Kong's* model armatures and

them being owned by different studios, the rumor seems less credible. When asked why spiders for both films had six legs, Farino chalks it up to cost cutting. "[It was] merely to simplify the animation, in the same way that Ray Harryhausen gave his 'octopus' in *It Came From Beneath the Sea* six tentacles and Mickey Mouse has only 3 fingers (and a thumb). That the spiders in both films each have six legs is a coincidence, not evidence," he said.

Adding to the trapdoor spider rumor is also the fact that Steve Archer claimed in his book *Willis O'Brien: Special Effects Genius* that it was the same model in a caption underneath a photo of items taken from a trunk belonging to Pete Peterson that contained some of O'Brien's old models (the trunk was later inherited by stop motion animator David Allen). However, that book came at a time when the flow of information was much different than it is today. "I attribute this to an assumption on Steve's part, just drawing a conclusion from seeing the spider model in that photo. Again, that the spider model was seen there is not, in itself, conclusive. Keep in mind that Steve's book was written in 1993; i.e., pre-internet, pre-Google, pre-email, and that Steve lived in England. As far as I know, he was not in direct contact with anyone in the field, and thus had no direct discussions on this matter," commented Farino. "I agree," said Wolf. "I don't want to rain on Steve Archer, but I don't think he had actual information. Look, Darlyne would have told me that if she'd known. Remember, the only photos that exist documenting the work on the pit are the ones she shared with us from her scrapbook. There was only a single slop print of a finished shot, though we know much, much more was filmed, including the use of live snakes as tentacles," he continued. On the claim that the beastie in the Peterson trunk originated with *Kong*, Wolf added, "I never heard Dave [Allen] say that and he and I discussed the topic of *Kong* many, many times." That being said, Wolf does think if any of the creatures in *The Black Scorpion* came from *Kong*, it would have been that one (although the circumstances make this unlikely). "If (big if), OBie had a puppet left over from *Kong* to recycle, I'd vote for the [spider] crab-thing as a candidate. We can see photos of it in some of Darlyne's behind-the-scenes pics and that is much, much closer to *The Black Scorpion* spider," he stated. (This was the previously mentioned model that was publicly displayed with a description saying that it was from *Kong*).

There have also been theories that the cave scene in *The Black Scorpion* may have been modeled after the scene in *Kong*. This also seems dubious, as the film's script was completed by the time O'Brien became involved. "He could very well have said, 'Hey, y'know, we once did a scene in *Kong* that was cut that would be the kind of thing that would fit in here perfectly.' [But] without specific information, it's often a slippery slope to assign or assume the authorship to specific ideas," remarked Farino.

Perhaps ironically, some items from *The Black Scorpion* were reused for later projects. One of the scorpion armatures was later repurposed by David Allen and Jim Danforth for the giant crab in *When Dinosaurs Ruled the Earth*. Wah Chang's big live action scorpion puppet went on to have parts used for one of the alien creatures in the 1964 *Outer Limits* episode "The Duplicate Man."

While it is impossible to be 100% certain as to whether the *Kong* models were reused or not, the evidence discussed renders it unlikely. "I'll conclude by saying that, admittedly, there is no specific, concrete, factual information that indicates anything one way or another. But given all of the factors; OBie didn't keep models, the models were the property of RKO, *The Black Scorpion* was made a quarter century after *Kong*, etc.; it's far more likely that OBie had new models made rather than go to the trouble of trying to acquire and license the *Kong* models only to have to refurbish them," stated Farino. "Again, Ernie is right on," agreed Wolf.

*This article would not have been possible without the generous participation of Ernest Farino and Mark Wolf. Mark Wolf's book *Smoke and Mirrors: Special Visual Effects B.C.* is expected to be out before the end of the year. The second volume, *The History and Technique of Fantasy Film Animation* will cover stop motion animation and is expected to be released some time in 2021.*

EVERY HORROR YOU'VE SEEN ON THE SCREEN GROWS PALE BESIDE THE HORROR OF....

THE BLACK SCORPION

DON'T BE ASHAMED TO SCREAM — IT HELPS TO RELIEVE THE TENSION!

FRANKENSTEIN MEETS THE WOLFMAN... AND TALKS!

Frankenstein Meets the Wolfman © 1943 Universal Pictures

The following article presents the rare case of a "lost film" that you can see...but can't hear. Perhaps that sounds a bit odd, but let me explain. As a kid, I always took note of the climax of *The Ghost of Frankenstein* (1942) wherein Ygor (Bella Lugosi) gets his brain implanted into the monster and then begins speaking. But then, in the follow-up, which was *Frankenstein Meets the Wolfman* (1943), the monster was silent yet again. And, he walked in a strange new manner, holding his arms out straight in front of himself. Initially, I just thought Universal didn't care about the continuity and retconned the idea of Ygor's brain in the monster's body.

As it turned out, I was wrong. The film's writer, Curt Siodmak, had not forgotten and wrote the monster still as Ygor, capable of speech. Worse still, the movie was shot as written with the monster speaking. And to really add insult to injury, Bela Lugosi actually played the monster for the first time! When the picture was screened, audiences laughed at Lugosi's Hungarian accent coming from the monster's mouth...which is a bit odd considering that's exactly what happens at the end of *Ghost of Frankenstein*. Universal executives didn't like it either and got cold feet. The film was re-edited to remove all shots of the monster talking. In cases where no replacement shots were available, shots of Lugosi moving his mouth were used, though his dialogue isn't dubbed in.

As such, there was once an entirely different version of *Frankenstein Meets the Wolfman* complete not only with extra dialogue, but entire extra scenes. In the 1980s, when Universal's horror films were being readied for VHS releases, an effort was made to find the original cut of *Frankenstein Meets the Wolfman* to no avail. Though it was laughed at in its day, modern film enthusiasts and grown-up "monster kids" might interpret the original cut differently. But we're getting ahead of ourselves.

The ending of *Ghost of Frankenstein* had Ygor's brain transplanted into the monster, an element not carried over into the final cut of *Frankenstein Meets the Wolfman.* Ghost of Frankenstein © 1942 Universal Pictures.

To start at the beginning, the whole concept was a joke cracked during lunch at the commissary. Siodmak wanted to make a joke to make his tablemates, Yvonne de Carlo and Mary MacDonald, laugh. As a producer, George Waggner, walked by their table, Siodmak made the following joke to him, "George, why don't we make a picture *Frankenstein Wolfs the Meat Man*—I mean *Frankenstein Meets the Wolfman.*"[1] The starlets laughed, but not Waggner. A few days later, the producer instructed Siodmak to write the very picture he suggested in jest!

Siodmak actually came up with a very solid storyline for the picture despite his skepticism for its potential.[2] Larry Talbot would revive from the grave. Discouraged,

he would seek out Dr. Frankenstein in an effort to end his life and, therefore, his curse. In his travels, he meets Ygor in the Frankenstein monster. Ygor wants just the opposite, to find Dr. Frankenstein so that he might live. The latter idea, due to the removal of Ygor's dialogue, isn't present in the final film at all.

Actually, on the note of Ygor and Bela Lugosi, initially, Lon Chaney Jr. was to play both the monster and Larry Talbot/the Wolf Man! If Universal had planned to have Lugosi at least read the monster's lines for continuity's sake is unknown. Either way, on October 14, 1942, *Variety* reported that, "Lon Chaney Jr. plays a double header as both Monsters in THE WOLF MAN MEETS FRANKEN-

"...no man has ever seen his like ... no woman ever felt his white-hot kiss ..."

Surpasses in THRILLS even DRACULA ... world's greatest hold-over picture for 1930 . . with

BELA LUGOSI

(Dracula himself)... as the leading spine-chiller ....

as a story it has thrilled the world for years.

Bela Lugosi was the first choice to play the monster in *Frankenstein* back in 1931, as evidenced in this early poster.

STEIN which goes to bat at Universal this week..."

Though executives felt that Chaney Jr. in both roles would make for extravagant publicity, it was decided that it may be too much stress for the sometimes erratic Chaney Jr. Even though he had played the monster in *Ghost of Frankenstein*, he loathed the makeup process, and asking him to play two monsters was a bit much. As such, Boris Karloff's name was brought up first. But Karloff had vowed to never play the monster again, and his voice sounded nothing like Lugosi's (not that the executives cared about such trivial matters). With some reluctance, it was decided to approach Lugosi

about playing the very role he had turned down over a decade ago. Ironically, one of the reasons Lugosi turned the role down in 1931 was that he would have no dialogue...

Lugosi, in desperate need of money, accepted the role of the Frankenstein monster. He would also have dialogue this time around, and in one sense would also be reprising the character of Ygor which he had played in the two previous Frankenstein films. Ironically in the final edit, not only would Lugosi not be heard, he also wasn't seen much. In reality the 60 year old actor was too old to adequately play the monster in full prosthetics. Most of the monster's scenes, or the more physically demanding ones anyways, were done by stuntmen Eddie Parker and Gil Perkins. IMDB's trivia section on the film says that in the end, Lugosi has only a little over five minute's worth of screen time, the other two minutes belonging to Parker and Perkins.

The script, entitled *Wolfman Meets Frankenstein* instead of the other way around, even has differences whereas Ygor/the Frankenstein monster are concerned. This is evident in the first scene, where the two thieves break into the Talbot crypt to steal Larry Talbot's valuables that he was allegedly buried with. As we all know, when

Colorized Lobby Card. *Frankenstein Meets the Wolfman* © 1943 Universal Pictures

the leaner thief goes to grab Talbot, who suspiciously hasn't decomposed at all, Talbot awakens and grabs the man! The script has the bulkier man escape the mausoleum as it burns down (his comrade's screaming figure shadow-lit by the flames), cutting himself on broken glass. His partner, caught in the grip of the undead Talbot, screams as he runs away. This was probably too intense for the time, and so the screaming and the blood were done away with (as were shots of the shadow reflected in the fire).

In both the film and the script, Talbot is next found unconscious in the streets and taken to a hospital. However, the script has a deleted scene of the police puzzling over Talbot's rotten decayed clothes, which they note were made in America. The film simply cuts straight to Talbot in a hospital bed being questioned and slowly regaining his memory. Among the men questioning him are Dr.

Manning, who we should note is named Dr. Harley in the script (why the name changed is unknown).

That night, alone in his room, the light of the moon strikes an agitated Talbot causing him to turn into the Wolf Man. Siodmak envisioned the scene differently, though, and wanted the transformation to take place in Talbot's sleep so that he would awaken as the Wolf Man. The following attack on the policeman is also slightly more elaborate in the script. Apparently censors must have had issues with screaming, for the policeman was meant to scream as the Wolf Man drags him away into the shadows. He utters no screams in the film, however.

The film follows the script pretty faithfully in the next scene, with Talbot trying to convince the police that he is a werewolf to no avail. Talbot then escapes (off-screen in both the film and the script) to go find the old gypsy woman, Maleva, from *The Wolf Man* (1941).

Siodmak's version of Talbot and

Deleted scenes of Talbot and Ygor/the monster warming up after being frozen in the ice.
Frankenstein Meets the Wolfman © 1943 Universal Pictures

Maleva's reunion is different. In the film it is friendlier and also includes an unscripted cameo for Chaney Jr.'s real life pet German Shepherd going up to great Talbot as he comes into camp. In Siodmak's script, Maleva is initially rude to Talbot and doesn't want to see him. In the film, Maleva is taken aback, but is still kind to Talbot.

As we all know, Maleva takes Talbot to the village of Vasaria to find Dr. Frankenstein, whom she is unaware has died. Depressed, the two ride away in their carriage when the moonlight strikes Talbot. In the film, he jumps out before he can even begin to change, but in Siodmak's script, Talbot and Maleva watch as his hands turn hairy before he jumps from the carriage. Offscreen (in the script and the film both) the Wolf Man kills a young woman, which incites the villagers

to seek vengeance. They chase the Wolf Man towards Frankenstein's castle. Siodmak's script has an extra scene where the Wolf Man hurls boulders at the mob from up the hill, but no such scene appears to have been shot. The Wolfman even dislodges a piece of castle wall and hurls it at the men before he falls into the bowels of the old castle. Presumably the scene wasn't shot due to time or budget constraints, because it surely would have thrilled audiences and it's a shame that it wasn't shot.

To move forwards a bit, the next morning, in human form, Talbot stumbles across the monster frozen in ice. In the final cut, we go from Talbot helping the monster out of

This scene, like so many others, was shot with Lugosi speaking dialogue, and cut later on. *Frankenstein Meets the Wolfman* © 1943 Universal Pictures

the ice to the duo walking through the ruins of the castle. "Dr. Frankenstein must have kept records...a diary. You know where it is, show me," Talbot says and the monster merely points ahead. Fans like myself were completely unaware that an entire sequence preceding this had already been deleted wherein the monster and Talbot had a lengthy conversation.

Originally—and these sequences were actually shot unlike some of the others (like the Wolfman throwing the boulders)—Talbot and the monster warm themselves around a fire. As the monster reaches his hand towards the fire, he says, "Where are you? I can hardly see..."

Talbot cautions him that his hands are too close to the flames and that he may burn himself.

"Burn myself..." the monster answers quizzically, and then asks Talbot to help him get up. Talbot does so and the monster explains that once he had the strength of "100 men" but now he has become ill.

As the duo walk through the castle, Siodmak does a very good job of establishing a bond between the two monsters. Ygor explains how he saw Ludwig Frankenstein die before his very eyes when the castle burned down. He also explains a chilling detail: while frozen in the ice he was in fact conscious but unable to move! Talbot sympathizes, having also been buried alive in his own way.

"Buried alive!...I know," Talbot says, which catches the monster's ear.

He asks Talbot what he is doing in the castle. When Talbot tells him that he is hiding, Ygor says, "Those futile little mortals! Do you hate them, too?"

Bitterly, Talbot responds with a yes, and Ygor states, "Then you are my friend...I need friends—so do you. We can help each other." And with this, the bond between the two monsters has a firm start.

The conversation continues, with Talbot revealing that he was looking for Dr. Frankenstein to help him die, while Ygor is ironically looking for him to live.

The dialogue is worth presenting in full:

> MONSTER: (sadly) If Dr. Frankenstein were still alive – he would restore my sight... He would give me back the strength I once possessed – the strength of a hundred men...so that I could live forever!
>
> LARRY: (aghast) Don't you ever want to die?
>
> MONSTER: Die? Never! Dr. Frankenstein created this body to be immortal!

I want to stop and point out that here Ygor recognizes that this is not his body, but that of the Frankenstein monster, a point that may have been lost on movie goers who hadn't seen or perhaps forgotten *The Ghost of Frankenstein*. However, as the dialogue continues, it becomes apparent that this may not be Ygor after all, but a strange fusion of Ygor and the monster, now one entity (or,perhaps, a split personality?).

> MONSTER: (continued) His son gave me a new brain, a clever brain. I shall use it for the benefit of the miserable people who inhabit the world, cheating each other, killing each other, without a thought but their own petty gains. I will rule the world! I will live to witness the fruits of my wisdom for all eternity.

That last bit of dialogue, however, sounds very much like something Ygor would say rather than the monster, implying this is indeed a fusion of the original monster and Ygor. This threat to take over the world also gives the story a totally different slant. The monster is now clearly a malevolent villain, rather than a dumb, tragic brute as presented in the final cut.

Talbot is too caught up in his own worries to take the monster's grandiose plans seriously. He tries to get the monster to see his side of things, giving him reasons and scenarios where he may wish to die as well one day. But the monster will entertain no such notion, boasting of how the "story of my creation" (notice how he said my creation, not the creation of the body) is written in Frankenstein's diary. He also says that in the same way that Frankenstein knew the secret of life, he also knew the secret of death—this catches Talbot's ear.

"The secret of death! He knew it—where is the book? I've got to have it!" Talbot shouts.

The monster asks why he should help him, still suspicious. Talbot, ever the smooth negotiator, reminds the monster that just as the book has the power to take his life, it can restore the monster from his weakened state. Talbot also adds in that the villagers may overpower him at some point. This gets the monster's attention, and he finally relents to show Talbot the diary.

From here, we come to the point that we see in the final cut of Talbot and the monster wandering through the castle. Only now I realize that in that scene Talbot isn't actually speaking (his lips do not move onscreen). When Talbot asks for the diary, that dialogue is actually looped in to clue we, the audience, in on what's going on since the original sequence containing that dialogue was removed. As we watch the scene, cognizant of the fact that the monster is Ygor, some interesting details are apparent. For instance,

ILONA MASSEY·LON CHANEY jr.·PATRIC KNOWLES · MARIA OUSPENSKAY · LIONE ATWILL

ILONA MASSEY · PATRIC KNOWLES
with
BELA LUGOSI · LIONEL ATWILL
MARIA OUSPENSKAYA
and LON CHANEY as THE WOLFMAN

FRANKENSTEIN
contro L'UOMO LUPO

directed by ROY WILLIAM NEILL

Top: Colorized Lobby Card. Bottom: Italian Poster. *Frankenstein Meets the Wolfman* © 1943 Universal Pictures

finding the secret compartment holding the notes—something the original monster would never do, but Ygor's would. Upon putting his hands on the lockbox, in the first cut he states, "Here it is."[3]

Talbot wrenches it excitedly from his hands and runs off to open it. In the final cut, as he follows Larry, we can see the monster's mouth moving, but no sound is coming out. In fact, Ygor is calling out to Talbot in fear that he has left him. In the final cut, we see Talbot open the box. Sadly for him, the notes are gone. "It isn't here," is all we hear Larry say, while the monster's mouth again moves with no sound. The monster is, in fact, saying, "Gone..."

Talbot then notices a picture on

the monster's hands are outstretched because he is blind and trying to find his way along—not because he is a dumb brute. The monster also visibly laughs upon the ground of Elsa Frankenstein. He reads the inscription on the photo and mutters, "Then she's the one that can tell me."

In reality, this is only half of the scene as originally shot. When he first finds nothing but bank notes in the lockbox, Talbot laments, "A diary...Are you sure this is where he kept it?"

The monster replies, "Yes – it was a book with brass clamps." The monster moves his hand through the box and mutters, "Gone..."

Talbot says, "The fire destroyed it..."

"It can't be," the monster replies, "it must not be..."

But then Talbot notices the photograph, picking it up and reading the inscription. "Elsa?" he mutters. "Did she die in the fire too?"

"No – I remember she escaped. She must still be alive."

This is then where Larry mutters the final line still present in the finished film. And with that, we fade to the real Elsa Frankenstein, set to meet Talbot under the impression that he is interested in buying her father's castle. When Talbot tells Elsa that he wants her father's notes, she says she doesn't know where they are, nor would she hand them over if she did. However, in the script, she takes pity on Talbot at the last moment and invites him to stay for the New Wine Festival. But, in the film, it is the mayor who invites Talbot to stay.

In the script, Talbot and Elsa have a conversation during the New Wine Festival about his reasons for wanting her father's research. She thinks he is a scientist, but he tells her he needs it because he is cursed. Before they can continue their discussion, a singing troupe comes upon them. In the movie, we follow the singers to Elsa and Talbot's table, there is no conversation between them, then Talbot has his outburst towards the singer in both versions. However, in the script the singer simply goes to the next table upon Talbot's rant, but in the film Talbot's outburst is enough to clear their section of the village square!

Dr. Mannering/Dr. Harley, the surgeon that operated on Talbot earlier, then comes onto the scene. Siodmak's dialogue for the duo is better than what was filmed. In the script, when Talbot asks him how he found him, Dr. Harley says, "I followed the cry of the wolf." In the film Manning just mentions following various newspaper clippings, there's no line about the wolf. Actually, in both versions the doctor merely thinks Talbot is a schizophrenic murderer, his line about the wolf's cry in the script was just a touch of unintentional irony. From here things play out similarly in both versions (the monster crashes the festival, and he and Talbot escape together on a covered wagon) with minor differences not worth discussing.

Not long after this is yet another deleted campfire scene between Talbot and the monster, who lays upon the ground with labored breath.

LARRY: Why did you come down to the village? Now they'll hunt us again –

The monster turns his ugly face towards the fire, beads of sweat on his forehead.

MONSTER: I was afraid you'd left me – I thought you'd found that diary – and run away –

Larry gets up. walks over to the enormous, prostrate body:

LARRY: (bitterly) You think you're so clever – Frankenstein gave you a cunning brain, did he? But you're dumb! You've spoiled our only chance –

Then the voices of Harley and Elsa can be heard in the distance and Talbot springs up to go find them.

"Don't leave me – don't go!" the monster wheezes. "I'm weak...They'll catch me and bury me alive!"

In the film, all we see is Talbot sitting at the fire, no monster in sight, when the trio of Harley, Elsa, and Maleva come calling. Talbot rushes out to meet them, and Elsa reveals that she is willing to help him find her father's diary. The monster hears the voices and picks up a piece of wood to defend himself with. "Steady!" Talbot yells as he approaches. "They're friends." The monster then puts down the wood.

Watching the scene in the film, one gets the impression that Talbot has tamed the monster as though he

were a pet. How could we know that this iteration of the monster was in fact an intelligent being? As originally shot, upon hearing Talbot's voice, Ygor/the monster says, "Oh, it's you."

In the final cut, as the scene continues, Talbot tells the seemingly dumb brute that, "This is Dr. Mannering, he's come to make you well."

Again, in the context of the final cut, it's weird that Talbot would bother to tell the monster the name of the doctor as opposed to just calling him a friend. And, what's wrong with the monster anyways? Because Ygor's dialogue was cut, we really don't know. Anyhow, in the film, upon hearing this, the monster turns to look at Dr. Mannering.

To avoid a shot of Lugosi speaking his dialogue, we cut to a shot of Elsa and Maleva watching from afar. Dr. Mannering's response to Ygor's cut dialogue is heard when he says, "Yes, that's why I'm here."

Again, in the context of this cut it

Frankenstein Meets the Wolfman © 1943 Universal Pictures

Frankenstein Meets the Wolfman © 1943 Universal Pictures

appears as though he's affirming what Talbot just said. But, in fact, he's affirming the monster's cut line which went, "To make me well – to give me back the strength of a hundred men?"

After the doctor's reply, both versions have him examine the monster. In another line of cut dialogue, Ygor said, "It's my eyes – I can scarcely see."

For a while, aside from trivial dialogue changes, the script and the film are the same, with Mannering/Harley manifesting a plan to drain Talbot's lifeforce and as well as that of the monster's (though Ygor thinks the doctor is here to help him).

The next significant scene to be altered again takes place around a fire. This time it is within the castle by a fireplace. The monster reclines against the wall in a white operating gown looking like a "Tibetan god", while Talbot paces the floor nervously. Talbot hears a strange noise and asks, "What was that?"

The monster answers, "The ice is melting...The water will be rushing down soon and turning the turbines...The machines will work again – and the doctor will make me strong once more."

The monster walks towards Talbot and continues, "Then I shall see again – and be fit to rule the world." As it turns out, this is the monster's last scripted line of dialogue.

Ironically, the fireplace scene was altered before it was even shot, as the final scene doesn't have the monster in an operating gown. And, it is Talbot who informs we, the audience, of the rushing waters preparing to power the turbines.

The script has an additional scene that may not have been filmed at all (as the monster doesn't speak, there's no reason to cut it necessarily). In it, Maleva brings Talbot a tray of food and he tells her that he can "feel the spell beginning" again. Maleva confirms that, indeed, it will be a full moon tonight. Talbot

ILONA MASSEY
LON CHANEY JR.
PATRIC KNOWLES
MARIA OUSPENSKAY
LIONE ATWILL

Frankenstein Meets the Wolfman © 1943 Universal Pictures

then rushes into the lab to beg Dr. Manning to do the procedure tonight—this is where we pick up in the film.

When Talbot leaves the room, Elsa mentions again how she thinks Talbot is insane. Maleva steps in to say, "Insane? He is not insane. He simply wants to die." The film cuts Maleva off here, but in the script, she also has an exchange with Elsa, who says, "Are you asking Doctor Harley to kill a man?"

Maleva responds, "It would not be murder...it would be an act of grace to deliver this unfortunate soul from the curse of such suffering."

Elsa and Harley stare at the old gypsy, who continues, "My powers have failed – but my prayers will be answered."

Later, in the script, as Harley reads the diary he learns how to depower the monster, so to speak. He also learns how to recharge the monster. Siodmak writes that "The muscles of [Harley's] face tighten and a mad gleam comes into his eyes." This is

meant to clue us in that something fishy is happening.

The film has Mannering clue us in as to what's happening via his exclamation to himself that, "I can't do it. I can't destroy Frankenstein's creation. I've got to see it at its full power."

In both versions, the doctor powers up the Frankenstein monster until he is stopped by Elsa. In the film she turns off a lever, but in the script her pleas cause Dr. Harley to come to his senses and realize just what a bad idea it is to revive the monster. Of course, it's too late, and before we know it the monster is bursting out of his restraints and Talbot is sprouting hair.

In the script, the Wolf Man breaks his restraints first and begins to approach the doctor and Elsa. The duo are saved by the Frankenstein monster, who wants to keep the doctor alive should he need him again. But, this is an odd choice in a way. Up to this point, the

ILONA MASSEY
LON CHANEY JR.
PATRIC KNOWLES
MARIA OUSPENSKAY
LIONE ATWILL

ROY WILLIAM NEILL **CONTRO**

Frankenstein Meets the Wolfman © 1943 Universal Pictures

monster/Ygor has been portrayed as a villain, and yet now he is saving the sympathetic protagonist (well, Elsa is a sympathetic protagonist at least). During shooting this was wisely reversed to have the monster burst free first and go after the humans. Though it makes no sense why Ygor would kill the doctor in this instance, it better plays into the monster being a villain. Or, perhaps the procedure has made the monster revert to his former self, and Ygor's brain has been fried in the process?

In either case, in the script Harley fights the Wolf Man off with a wrench, while in the film he fights off the monster the same way. In the film, the monster then picks up Elsa and carries her off. The Wolf Man breaks free and goes after the monster.

The fight ends in a draw due to the actions of a supporting character named Vazec, who has rigged the dam with dynamite. He lights the fuse and the dam explodes, sending a rushing torrent at the titular monster, fighting away in the lab.

As to how much the final battle differs between the film and the script, that's hard to say. Basically, Siodmak didn't write much for the fight, perhaps knowing that it would be choreographed by someone else anyway, so why bother? Siodmak did envision a different ending for the human protagonists. While the film drops the ball where Maleva is concerned, in the script she was to take her horse and buggy towards the castle to rescue Harley and Elsa. The duo come running outside just as the flood waters are released. Harley gets into Maleva's buggy with Elsa, and the trio ride away to safety.

They make it back to Vasaria, and with the villagers, watch the disaster unfold. Siodmak envisioned it to be an epic scene, where the flood caused a roaring wind and a dust storm that would obscure the mountains. As the villagers watch this, Maleva rides

swirling vortex. Here, Siodmak wished for the film to end and fadeout.

And just how much did the deletion of Lugosi's lines affect the film? Quite a bit, it could be argued. The final battle in the context of the script and in the film is entirely different due to the removal of the subplot regarding Ygor planning to one day rule the world. This actually made the monster the villain and Larry/the Wolf Man the hero in a way. Or, in other

away. As the dust settles, "the outline of a new hill can be seen. Where the ruins stood, there is now a huge tomb of earth and rocks, covering the grave of the two phantoms."

Siodmak envisioned the moon disappearing behind the hill, and then we would have dissolved to one final shot. A page of Frankenstein's diary floats atop the water, and is then sucked into a

words, the Wolf Man was the monster you were supposed to root for in the climax. After all, if he lost, the monster might take over the world! But, with this subplot deleted, the film's ending is shaded with a bit of tragedy. It seems that the "innocent, dumb monster" is fighting his "friend" the Wolf Man. In a strange way, both versions have their merits, different though they may be.

---

[1] Siodmak, *Universal Filmscripts Series, Classic Horror Films – Vol. 5*, pp.8.
[2] Siodmak made it a practice of his to write in a ludicrous scene just to see if the producers read his scripts all the way through or not. His test this outing was a scene where Larry Talbot, dressed in a three piece suit, walks along the road with the monster. He tells him, "You know, I turn into a wolf by night." Ygor's reply, "Are you kiddin'?" [Siodmak, *Universal Filmscripts Series, Classic Horror Films – Vol. 5*, pp.9.]
[3] Actually, in 2010, YouTuber Cynthia Levin took the time to remove the background music from the scene and Lugosi can still be heard speaking!

BLOOD FROM THE MUMMY'S TOMB

STARRING PETER CUSHING & DIRECTED BY SETH HOLT

Blood from the Mummy's Tomb © 1971 Hammer Films

By 1970, it had been three years since Hammer's last Mummy movie, that being *The Mummy's Shroud* from 1967. James Carreras began itching for another Mummy film and ordered a new screenplay. Unfortunately, no one knows what the 1970 pitch entailed. All we know is that it was to be co-written and directed by Jimmy Sangster. See the letter written by Anthony Hinds to Jimmy Sangster on April 17, 1970, below:

Dear Jimmy: Jim Carreras has asked me to write a 'Mummy' script. I gather that Hammer was pleased with your performance as director [on *Horror of Frankenstein*]: If you have been bitten by the bug and fancy doing more of it, maybe you'd like to work on the script with me. You will appreciate I have no influence at Hammer anymore,[1] so this is not a contract!"[2]

Talks didn't last long. James

Carreras canceled the production on April 22nd when he failed to garner any interest from investors. He sent the following letter to Sangster:

Dear Jimmy. I have today told Tony Hinds that there is very little interest in a MUMMY subject. Under the circumstances, therefore, we will have to forget it.[3]

The lack of interest wasn't necessarily surprising. Of all Hammer's monster properties, the mummy films were the least sexy of the bunch at a time when sex was selling Hammer's films to a greater extent. True, cleavage had always been an aspect of Hammer horror, but 1970's *The Vampire Lovers* had featured an abundance of nudity and had been a sizeable hit. By comparison, the mummy was kid stuff. Perhaps then, it should come as no surprise that it took a pretty girl to sell the next Hammer mummy film.

Later in 1970, press agent Howard Brandy pitched to James Carreras the idea of adapting Bram Stoker's 1903 novel *Jewel of the Seven Stars*. Often obscured by the shadow of Stoker's seminal *Dracula*, *Seven Stars* concerned an archeologist's efforts to revive the ancient Egyptian mummy, Queen Tera, whom he has fallen in love with. Brandy told Ted Newsom in an interview that he gave Carreras a brief outline of the story and that Carreras loved it. "It's a mummy movie with a pretty girl, and [Carreras] immediately said yes."[4]

As Hammer had a three-picture deal already set up with EMI, the *Jewel of the Seven Stars* adaptation became one of those projects. However, Carreras disliked that title and felt it would fare better with "Mummy" in the title. After all, it had an Egyptian aspect to it, so why not? Specifically, according to Christopher Wicking, Carreras scrambled all the keywords relating to Mummy movies like "blood," "shroud," "tomb," etc. and came up with *Blood from the Mummy's Tomb* (though "Bosoms from the Mummy's Tomb" may have been more appropriate).

Wicking's first draft of the screenplay was entitled *Bram Stoker's Blood from the Mummy's Tomb* and was "unusable" according to Howard Brandy. According to Brandy, the draft was very short, had several explicit nude scenes (that were later removed), and when asked to do a rewrite, Wicking refused. Wicking, on the other hand,

Two stills of Peter Cushing as Professor Fuchs with Valerie Leon as Margaret. The scene they are filming is the one where Fuchs gives his daughter Tera's ring as a birthday present. © 1971 Hammer Films

claimed that Brandy had a falling out with his agent and that this was the cause of the drama. Whatever the case, the chosen director (recommended by Wicking himself) was Seth Holt, who had directed *The Nanny* (with Bette Davis) for Hammer in 1965.[5] In addition to being short,.

Though *Blood from the Mummy's Tomb* was completed, it should have ended up as a very different film if not for several unfortunate tragedies. Following the drama with Wicking, there was an actor's strike that threatened to hold up the

production, among other things. However, two tragic deaths impacted the project irrevocably: that of director Seth Holt's and Peter Cushing's wife, Helen Cushing.

The first day of shooting comprised of the scene where Professor Fuchs, as currently played by Cushing, gifted Tera's ring to his daughter Margaret on her birthday. Filming was slow due to Leon's inexperience, so not much was shot.[6]

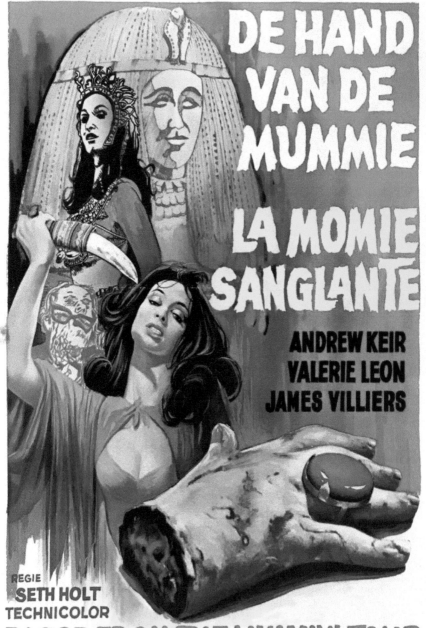

EXCELSIOR FILMS

DE HAND VAN DE MUMMIE

LA MOMIE SANGLANTE

ANDREW KEIR
VALERIE LEON
JAMES VILLIERS

REGIE
SETH HOLT
TECHNICOLOR

BLOOD FROM THE MUMMY'S TOMB

Christopher Neame, the production manager, remembered in issue #20 of *The House That Hammer Built* that the crew was aware that Helen Cushing was sick. As such, shooting was scheduled around Cushing so that he could not only get all of his scenes out of the way in general, but also leave early each day of shooting. "We wanted him to have as much time as he could with her and we'd planned to work with him primarily and get rid of him during the day as soon as possible."[7]

After the first day of shooting was over, that night, the second assistant director called Cushing to let him know the schedule for the next day. Cushing informed him that, tragically, Helen was not expected to make it through the night. She didn't, and Hammer knew Cushing wouldn't be able to finish the film. With only one day's worth of footage shot, it was decided that it would be easiest to recast Cushing. Hammer did so in only one day, getting Andrew Keir to play the role of Fuchs.[8]

Keir recalled the incident in an interview with Stephen Laws at the Manchester Festival of Fantastic Films in 1993. Keir said that

Carreras called him on a Friday night to inform him of the tragedy of Helen Cushing, and asked if he could take on Peter's part in the film. Keir, a good sport, traveled overnight to Wales without even having read the script to join shooting. Keir remembered, "Peter had marvelous qualities and as the part was written for Peter, it could only really be Peter in that role."[9]

In an interview Leon recalled her sadness at not being able to work further with Cushing. When interviewed by Tim Greaves in *Little Shoppe of Horrors* #12, she said:

"We actually did shoot the scene when he gives me the ring right at the beginning of the film, I remember that very well. And I was really sad when he had to drop out. Not only is he a really nice man, but obviously better known that Andrew Keir."[10]

Four weeks later, the next major tragedy occurred when Holt dropped dead of what was presumed to be a heart attack. Again, the production was faced with a seemingly insurmountable obstacle. Shooting had progressed far enough that it wouldn't be worth it to reshoot the whole film. Don Sharp, who had directed *Kiss of the Vampire* in 1963, was considered but it would end up being Michael Carreras himself who stepped in to finish the job.

During a telephone interview conducted by John Hamilton with Christopher Neame on April 3, 2010, Hamilton asked Neame just how different he thought the film would have been had Cushing played Fuchs and Holt had finished directing/editing.

Neame said, "It would have been better. I have always found Peter Cushing a more watchable actor than Andrew Keir, who did a good job, but Peter was a bigger name."[11]

There were other reasons behind Neame's statement as well. For starters, Holt didn't keep editorial notes. "[Holt would] shoot certain things and I'd ask, 'Why are you shooting that?'" remembered Neame. "He'd say, 'Don't worry, I know what I'm going to do with that. I can't wait to get my hands on this in the editing room.'"[12] Also, Holt's death meant that his usual editor, Oswald Hafenrichter, wouldn't be working on the film (actually, because Carreras fired Hafenrichter).

Carreras himself recalled the problems with taking up for Holt, stating that the main one was that Holt had shot the main portion of many scenes—just not the characters entering and exiting! Therefore Carreras had to restage many scenes to complete the task. Nor was any effort made by Carreras to emulate Holt's style according to some, though Carreras told *Fangoria* that he "tried to copy Seth's work as much as possible."[13]

Despite its setbacks, the film was received better by critics than many previous Hammer films had been in the past and is fondly remembered today by many as "the second-best Hammer Mummy film" behind the 1959 original.

---

[1] Anthony Hinds had sold off his interest in Hammer by 1970.

[2] Hallenbeck, Bruce G. "The Making of the Hammer Classic *Blood from the Mummy's Tomb*." *Little Shoppe of Horrors* #24. pp. 84.

[3] Ibid.

[4] Ibid, pp.85.

[5] Before Holt, Gordon Hessler and Peter Duffell were considered.

[6] Furthermore, before the casting of Valeri Leon, Carreras wanted another woman to play the part: Deborah Grant, a performer in the Royal Shakespear Company. Grant recalled in an interview with Jonathon Sothcott that she did a screen test for the film with Valerie Leon. She recalled that she wore Elizabeth Taylor's costume from *Cleopatra*. According to Grant, Leon won out due to her "frontage". This would appear to be true, as Leon had very little in the way of acting skills. Furthermore, her real voice isn't even heard in the film. She was, in fact, dubbed by a "middle-aged actress" whose name isn't given.

[7] Neame as quoted in "The Making of the Hammer Classic *Blood from the Mummy's Tomb*." Little Shoppe of Horrors #24, pp. 89.

[8] This wasn't the first time that Keir replaced Cushing. He also did so on *Dracula, Prince of Darkness*, as the early drafts featured Van Helsing until it was learned that Cushing was unavailable. Therefore, a new character was created for Keir: Father Sandor.

[9] Hallenbeck, Bruce G. "The Making of the Hammer Classic *Blood from the Mummy's Tomb*." *Little Shoppe of Horrors* #24, pp. 90.

[10] Ibid.

[11] Hamilton, "Christopher Neame Interview," *Little Shoppe of Horrors* #24, pp.82.

[12] Ibid, pp.93.

[13] Ibid, pp.94.

TERROR IN THE STREETS

TURNS 50
BY
MAXWELL
BRESEE

to direct both simultaneously. Unreleased on home video even in its native Japan (and only sparingly airing on television), the film has recently been translated via fan efforts for everyone to see.

The plot concerns a young woman named Yuri (played very well by starlet Wakako Sakai, who's just about the spitting image of innocence) who's been having a very bad week – she's laid off her temp job for no discriminable reason, is dumped by her boyfriend, forced to move out of her apartment, gets an application rejected, is robbed and is accused of robbing after taking a sleazy hostess job out of desperation. This string of bad luck is enough to drive her to the breaking point. But there seems to be an unnerving presence looming at every step she takes, meaning somebody must be behind all of this. But just who and why?

To describe the plot in much more detail would lead to spoilers, but suffice to say, it gets pretty wild to the point of utter confusion. But that's not a negative, as Yuri is completely in the dark about just what is happening until the very end. You are in her shoes for the

Terror in the Streets (黄昏の悪魔 *Tasogare no Akuma* lit. *The Devil Calls*) is a 1970 psychological thriller based on the book *The Devil of Twilight* (黄昏の悪魔 *Tasogare no Akuma*) by Kikuo Tsunoda, directed by Michio Yamamoto, (best known internationally for his "Bloodthirsty" Trilogy of Vampire films) and released on double-bill with his *The Vampire Doll*. Indeed, two movies from not only the same director but featuring almost entirely the same crew (most notably cinematographer Kazutami Hara and composer Riichiro Manabe) released together is pretty unusual, but this was apparently done by Tomoyuki Tanaka as a favor to Yamamoto – they wanted a traditional horror film in-vein to Hammer, but he wanted to direct a more Hitchcockian thriller. As a result, they gave him the greenlight

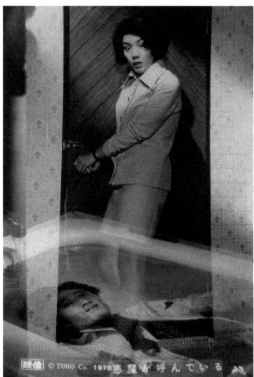

Terror in the Streets © 1970 Toho Co., Ltd.

This critique of how women are often treated as objects as opposed to actual people is further exemplified by the way in which the various kidnappers treat Yuri (with the lone female kidnapper being the only one with a dose of sanity/empathy) and is only solidified once we finally meet and learn the motivations of the culprit behind everything.   If anything, it's just a shame Yuri's "savior", the handsome office worker Urabe, wasn't a woman.

Even if it's a bit jumbled from a story perspective,   the movie is still very solid on a technical level. As to be expected, Yamamoto's direction is eerie and suspenseful, helped largely by Hara's cinematography. The title sequence has shots of crowds and pollution in an industrial city that would feel right at home in *All Monsters Attack*, *Godzilla vs. Hedorah* and *Godzilla vs. Gigan* (which is ironic considering *Terror in the Streets* features Kubota [the alien villain of *Gigan*] himself, Toshiaki Nishizawa). Manabe's score, like that for the Bloodthirsty movies and *Hedorah* and *Megalon* is an unusual but memorable one that fits quite well with the chaotic nature of the movie.

I've always been fascinated by the more obscure entries in Toho's catalog of Special Effects films (via listings on sites like Toho Kingdom), and *Terror* became somewhat of a "holy grail" for a period of time.

whole movie, and as stated, Wakako Saki does a very good job in the role. You desperately want to see her escape all of this madness. If there's one takeaway you'll have, it's that money truly is the root of all evil.

Though perhaps unintentional, the film may have a bit to say about how women were and still are treated in society. Yuri's status as a temporary employee was often enforced upon working women in Japan, given the chance they could fall in love, get married and have children, therefore outliving their "usefulness". The nightclub where she takes the hostess job forces its women to be mere sexualized objects (with one guest groping a woman trying to guess her bra size), with the owner telling Yuri not to dress like a "Kindergarten teacher".

With such a generic title and poster, just what could the movie be about? The description provided by Toho for their sales catalogs lists it being about a woman stalked by an invisible man. Some publications feature an image of Wakako Sakai posing with a wax mannequin of the Wolf Man (possibly taken during production of the movie), labeling it as a still from the film and leading some to believe said mannequin is a monster that appears in it. Despite occasionally being listed alongside Toho's science fiction/fantasy outputs, there is nothing supernatural in the movie at all. Of course, that shouldn't turn anybody away from the movie.

The creepy orcania music, cinematography and sheer craziness of the situation still give the movie an otherworldly feel that doesn't make it out of place alongside Toho's more horror-oriented special effects offerings. While perhaps not an undiscovered masterpiece, *Terror in the Streets* is a solid little thriller that keeps viewers on the edge of their seats wondering what will happen next. It and *The Vampire Doll* back-to-back must have made for a great time at the movies. And with subtitles now available (funded by yours truly), there's never been a better time to check it out!

BRIDE OF GODZILLA'S

65TH UNNIVERSARY

©東宝

Above: This Japanese Bromide Card depicts Rodan as an Archaeopteryx, which is what he was in concept art and maquette form. Rodan © 1956 Toho Co, Ltd. **Right: One of the aliens in this photo is Hideo Unagami, though we don't know which.** The Mysterians © 1957 Toho Co., Ltd.

Since Godzilla's birth over sixty years ago in 1954, there have been over thirty Godzilla films. That's fairly common knowledge. But what you may not know is that there are just about that many unmade Godzilla movies as well. The first, and most infamous of these shall always be 1955's *Bride of Godzilla*. In the bonkers storyline, an inventor named Dr. Shida has constructed a giant robot made in the image of his first love, who has married another man. Making matters even stranger, the giant robot is also naked (though I would assume "naked" in the Barbie doll sense). The movie would end with Godzilla and the giant robot wrestling about a city until Godzilla becomes enamored with the giant woman. He carries her off to his underwater cave, and the bride detonates a secret atomic bomb

within her body, thus entombing herself and Godzilla underground... until the next sequel.

This storyline was meant to follow 1955's *Godzilla Raids Again*. It would not only have brought back Godzilla and Anguirus, but would have introduced an as of yet unnamed version of Rodan. And, that's the funny thing about *Bride of Godzilla*. A good portion of the story deals with miners in Kyushu discovering a prehistoric cavern within the earth. Said cavern is the home of a giant Archaeopteryx (the Rodan proto-type), Anguirus, Godzilla, mermaids (!) and giant insects.

Bride of Godzilla was written in 1955. *Rodan*, which features Kyushu miners discovering a hidden cavern of horrors (complete with giant bugs and birds), was released in 1956. That's no coincidence. What is strange is that the man who wrote *Bride of Godzilla* got no credit on *Rodan*. He was a bit part actor named Hideo Unagami, who actually appeared in *Rodan*. Unagami also portrayed one of the aliens in *The Mysterians* (1957). Actor Yoshio Tsuchiya (the Mysterian commander) once made the claim that one of the actors alongside of him had a horrible allergic reaction to the make-up used to portray the Mysterians, and that the man died! Presumably Tsuchiya spoke of Unagami, who tragically died in 1957. Sadder yet, Unagami died the day after Toho producer Tomoyuki Tanaka

greenlit a sci-fi story he wrote. The story would be completed and released in 1958 as *The H-Man*.

Odder still, in 1977, Tanaka dusted off the old *Bride* script to serve as the official series reboot! Three versions of the story were created, one of which featured a flesh and blood female Godzilla as the titular Bride à la *King Kong Lives* (1986). Eventually, throughout seven years' worth of revisions, the project did turned into *The Return of Godzilla* (1984)/*Godzilla 1985*. And, the beginning scene featuring a giant mutated sea louse originated all the way back in 1955's *Bride of Godzilla*...

LOST FILMS REBORN!!!!

Since the publication of the book *Toho Tokusatsu Unpublished Works* in 2010 (all about unmade Toho SPFX films), fans have rallied to make their own versions of these "lost films" in their own unique ways from comic books to radio dramas (all of which are non-profit, just-for-fun projects, it should be noted). Here is a rundown on the more notable efforts...

THE MAKING OF
BATMAN MEETS GODZILLA
BY ERIC ELLIOTT

For more than 50 years, *Batman Meets Godzilla* remained a forgotten, lost movie project. The only concrete evidence of the unmade movie sat in the vaults of the University of Wyoming's William Dozier archive as a movie treatment, featuring the Adam West Batman and the Showa Era Godzilla. Dozier produced the 1966 *Batman* TV Series, but no one knows how the project started or why it never materialized.

The lost movie first came to my attention in 2019 through an interview with Batman historian

and artist, Chip Kidd, on Gilbert Gottfried's Amazing Colossal Podcast. The show's co-host, Frank Santopadre, asked Kidd if he was familiar with *Batman Meets Godzilla*. Kidd, who recently completed two Japanese related Batman works (the fantastic Bat-Manga! and Batman Collected) never heard of the project. Incredibly, this project remained unknown, even to serious Batman historians.

As a child growing up in the late 1970's, I loved the *Batman* TV series. The 1966 show aired in syndication so I got to watch the adventures of the Dynamic Duo every day after school. Godzilla also featured large in my childhood, having both a Saturday morning cartoon and a jumbo Shogun Warrior. So when I heard about *Batman Meets Godzilla*, I raced to my computer to learn more.

I read everything I could find on the movie, including John LeMay's invaluable *The Big Book of Japanese Giant Monster Movies: The Lost Films*. As unbelievable as it sounded, in the late 1960's, *Batman Meets Godzilla* was a real possibility. Following the success of *King Kong vs. Godzilla*, Toho Co. kicked around several ideas for the next Godzilla movie, including *Frankenstein vs. Godzilla*. At the same time, the *Batman* TV Series prepared a global assault on the airwaves, including Japan.

Leading up to the show's debut in January 1966, Japanese companies prepared new toys and Manga to capitalize on the popularity of the Caped Crusaders. It is not hard to imagine, that in the buzz leading up to the show's debut, Toho Co. considered Batman as a ready rival or at least a campy cohort to invigorate their waning Godzilla.

The treatment itself offers very few clues about its origins. Just a mere twenty-one pages long, the treatment offers a basic roadmap for a fun-filled, silly, sometimes weird showdown between our favorite franchises. No author is listed, although handwritten notes mark the pages.

One theory is that Godzilla series writer, Shinichi Sekizawa, wrote the treatment himself. There are even photos that purport to be pages of a Japanese treatment written by Sekizawa. Could the treatment found in the William Dozier archive

be an English translation of the Sekizawa treatment?

To me the treatment reads like it could have originated from a Japanese author. The author seems more familiar with the landmarks and culture of Japan than the hallmarks of a good Batman adventure.

For instance, while the TV show mostly drew its antagonists from Batman's colorful rogue's gallery, the treatment instead features a generic German mad scientist type. The treatment also omits Alfred Pennyworth, Bruce Wayne's steadfast butler and friend. The treatment also commits the cardinal sin of excluding a death trap. Perhaps the strongest evidence for Sekizawa's involvement though, is the use of a plot point that would make it into a later Godzilla movie — a weather control device.

However strong the evidence for a Japanese author is, there are still some nagging issues that suggest at least some involvement from Dozier's team. For instance, Batgirl features prominently in the movie treatment but the character does not appear in the TV series until the third season. Outside of Dozier's team, few people would have known about this character at the time the treatment was written. Unfortunately, we may never know the truth.

However it originated and for whatever reason it remained unmade, the movie deserved a life. Just the idea of Batman in Tokyo matching up against the "King of Monsters" filled me with inspiration. I thought it might be possible to crowd source a comic book adaptation of the treatment.

Fellow fan and artist, Brian Richard, directed me to the location of the treatment at the University of

Wyoming. A day later I had a pdf of the treatment. I spent a few weeks digesting the treatment and developing an outline for a comic book. I wanted to be faithful to the treatment as much as possible while attempting to please both the Batman and Godzilla fans with additional elements from those franchises.

From the Batman franchise, I brought in the villain Professor Hugo Strange, whose mind-control powers and mad scientist vibe fit the bill. I also added a significant part for Alfred Pennyworth. Finally, I felt the story needed more Bat gadgets and vehicles to feel like an authentic 1960's Batman story.

From the Godzilla movies, I added the terrorist organization, Red Bamboo, who featured in the 1966 film, *Ebirah, Horror of the Deep*. I also added references and plot points featuring other Kaiju like Mothra.

Once I had a script together, I enlisted the help of my friend and creator of the MASK '86 comic, Kero Wack, to draw a cover for the first issue. With the cover in hand, I reached out to other comic book artists and writers on social media to bring the project to life.

I honestly was not sure if anyone would be interested. But to my great surprise, within a week I had more than twenty volunteers who answered the call. I credit Kero Wack's outstanding cover for giving the project enough credibility to get off the ground.

The volunteers signed on for many different reasons. Some were Batman fans like artists Ian Miller and Howard Simpson. Some were huge Godzilla fans like artist, Stephen Schilling and writer Matt Dennion. Some volunteers just wanted to be part of a group project like artist Josue Cubero. The volunteers joined from all over the world including Egypt, Costa Rica, Australia, and England.

We are now two issues into a three-issue comic book adaption. We are grateful for the online support from Batman and Godzilla fans. Because at the end of the day, this is a fan project; made by fans for fans. Read the *Batman Meets Godzilla* comic book adaptation at www.batmanmeetsgodzilla.com.

Follow us on Twitter or like us on Facebook and you'll have a chance to win *Batman Meets Godzilla* t-shirts and other prizes.

Eric Elliott is an author and blogger. His upcoming projects include a return to the Batman of the Tim Burton films. Follow him on Twitter.

AN INTERVIEW WITH THE CREATORS OF

GODZILLA UNMADE

In the summer of 2020, the Kaijusaurus Podcast adapted three very unique, un-produced Godzilla stories into short audio dramas.

SS: Steven Sloss (project director, project editor, writer of *Godzilla vs. the Last Gargantua*)
RC: Raffael Coronelli (writer of *Godzilla vs. Hedorah II*)
DS: Daphne Sharp (writer of *Bride of Godzilla?*)

1. Before we get started, there's a lot to commend you all for. First off, you managed to capture the essence of what were sometimes full scripts into a relatively short (less than 20 minutes) audio play. Second, the music and sound effects you chose were amazing, and even the voice actors capture the essence of dubbers from the 50s and the 70s. What was your inspiration for producing them as audio dramas?

SS: I think a lot of people tend to think of the kaiju genre as a purely visual experience. A lot of fans focus on the thrill of *seeing* monsters destroy cities, battle each other, fend off military forces, etc. But anyone that grew up on Toho's science fiction films will know that there's absolutely nothing else on Earth that *sounds* like them. Beyond the roars of monsters themselves, any fan can instantly recognize the sound of a Toho Maser canon, a tank firing, a rocket taking off, a building collapsing, and especially an explosion. Realizing this gave me an idea. I listen to a lot of audio and radio dramas, and am a big fan of

the production company Big Finish, who produce audio dramas based on licensed cult properties like *Doctor Who*, *Torchwood*, and *Dark Shadows*, among others. I realized I had the opportunity to do with Godzilla what Big Finish has done for so many other cult properties, as well as give Godzilla fans a new, unique way to experience kaiju fiction.

2. Why did you pick the following three stories to adapt? (*Godzilla vs. the Last Gargantua, Godzilla vs. Hedorah II, Bride of Godzilla?*) Did you feel they were the easiest to condense or were they simply your favorites?

SS: *Last Gargantua* is probably the loosest adaptation of the bunch, since it's not really an adaptation of anything in particular beyond a suggestion by Henry G. Saperstein and Reuben Bercovtich. I always felt the ending of *The War of the Gargantuas* was open-ended, and suggested more Gargantua creatures could emerge in the following years. That was my primary motivation for choosing this particular pitch. I knew from the start I also wanted to produce an adaptation of Yoshimitsu Banno's *Godzilla vs. Hedorah II* pitch, as the idea of bringing to life another of Banno's ideas was irresistible. And as for *Bride*, it was actually Raffael who suggested that one.

RC: When Steven conceived of the project, there were a few titles he had in mind that he wanted us to adapt. One of them was *Godzilla vs. Hedorah II*, and it took me about one second to jump at that one. Of the three, it was the one that I felt the most strongly about, since Yoshimitsu Banno's three-decade-plus endeavor to bring some iteration of that movie to the screen was something I'd known about for a long time. I saw Banno-sensei in person at G-fest years ago, in a talk he gave about his plan to make *Godzilla 3D to the Max* — which itself would've been a reworked version of the rematch between Godzilla and Hedorah (now renamed Deathla). Banno's stylistic invention and strong thematic language was something I was excited to channel in my own version of the story, and it fit with a couple original ideas I ended up throwing in there.

DS: Steven chose me to adapt *Bride* into a script, and if we did things all over again I'd definitely still want to tackle that story. I saw a Jules Verne-esque adventure story amongst the weirdness, and I had so much fun bringing it to life. I also figured I could take a very strange premise and make it fun while excising the more uncomfortable implications of the original plot.

3. What were the runners up that you also considered but ultimately didn't go with?

SS: Funnily enough, I didn't really consider any others beyond the three we produced. One caveat I gave myself in selecting lost projects to produce was that I didn't want to adapt anything that ended up being produced in one shape or another, so that ruled out pitches like *King Kong vs. Ebirah* (becoming *Ebirah, Horror of the Deep*) and *Godzilla vs. Redmoon* (eventually produced as *Daigoro vs. Goliath*). I also saw no point in producing audio dramas based on earlier versions of eventually-produced scripts, like the well-known initial draft of *Godzilla, Mothra, and King Ghidorah: Giant Monsters All-Out Attack*, which featured Anguirus and Varan. I also didn't want to produce anything featuring the cutting-room kaiju Bagan.

4. I was most impressed with *Godzilla vs. Hedorah II*. There was no actual script for that (other than that it would be set in Africa), but I can tell what you did was take inspiration from Yoshimitsu Banno's other works to flesh it out. Was setting the story in South America rather than Africa a nod to *Godzilla 3-D to the Max* (this was a quasi-sequel to *Godzilla vs. Hedorah* set partially in South America).

RC: Changing the location to South America was absolutely an homage to *Godzilla 3D*. That version of the movie was one that I'd followed during its attempted production, so I'm glad our take on it could include some reference to it.

5. What about the mutated cannibalistic natives, I take it that was lifted from *Prophecies of Nostradamus* (1974)?

RC: *Prophecies of Nostradamus* was a major influence for not only the Italian exploitation style cannibal scenes (set of course to Fabio Frizzi's *Cozilla* theme as a kind of tangential homage to Fulci's *Zombi*

2), but the overall tone. When Banno wrote the script for *Nostradamus*, he was angry — fed up — in a state of mind similar to what a lot of us are feeling at this very grim moment in history (the year 2020). Channeling it for Hedorah's resurgence just made sense.

SS: I'm a big fan of Italian genre films too, so getting the opportunity to marry these two cult genres in an elegant, natural way was irresistible.

6. *Spoiler Alert* At the drama's end, Godzilla flies high into the skies to take Hedorah away and doesn't appear to return to Earth. This is similar to another unmade movie, *Gamera vs. Phoenix*, where Gamera flies away from earth never to return again. Was that the inspiration?

RC: I actually wasn't familiar with *Gamera vs. Phoenix*. I've always just felt like blasting off into space like a Saturn V rocket is something Godzilla should be able to do. It makes sense to me, and I think it would to Banno-sensei as well. He's leaving this planet that's treated him badly and getting away from all our crap. Will he ever come back? As Doctor Yanno says, "who can tell?"

7. In your other dramas, you use some familiar Akira Ifukube and Masaru Sato tracks, but in *Godzilla vs. Hedorah II*, you lifted tracks from a Riichiro Manabe score (Manabe scored *Godzilla vs. Hedorah*), what film is it from? Is it *Terror in the Streets*?

SS: In *Hedorah II*, I used some Manabe tracks from his two Godzilla scores (*Godzilla vs. Hedorah* and *Godzilla vs. Megalon*),

but there are also tracks lifted from *Terror in the Streets* and *Lake of Dracula*, two '70s Toho horror movies directed by Michio Yamamoto and scored by Manabe. I wanted listeners to instantly recognize Manabe's distinct scoring style, while using some less familiar, more sinister tracks of his. I think they suit the tone of Raffael's piece very well, and help cement the feeling of a lost Yoshimitsu Banno kaiju film.

8. *Spoiler alert!* *Godzilla vs. the Last Gargantua* features a red, steaming "Titan" variety of Gargantua named Yogara. I only recently saw *Attack on Titan* parts I & II and loved them. I take it that was an inspiration behind Yogara, since aspects of *Attack on Titan* were themselves inspired by *War of the Gargantuas*?

SS: Absolutely. Since seeing Shinji Higuchi's live action *Attack on Titan* movies, the temptation to produce something that married them with *Frankenstein Conquers the World* and *The War of the Gargantuas* was too much to resist. That's what eventually led to *Godzilla vs. the Last Gargantua*, throughout which I tried to weave clues as to Yogara's – the "last Gargantua" – true identity, culminating in Dr. Paul Stewart's final line in the finished drama.

9. How challenging was it to adapt *Bride of Godzilla*, which had a full screenplay, not to mention some really wacky elements?

DS: I had the unintentional benefit of not knowing a full screenplay existed when I started writing the *Bride* script — I didn't learn about it until a few hours before the finished episode came out! In the end, having only a few basic elements (a line of dialogue, the robot with a woman's face who 'seduced' Godzilla, the Hollow Earth monsters and mermaids) helped me create a more streamlined script without any real issues. The biggest challenge was keeping the script in line with the dialogue in the Showa dubs I grew up on — if a line didn't sound like it could have come from one of my old VHS dubs, I rewrote it until it sounded right in my head. Including all the weird, wild stuff and coming up with Alice and Kasumi was probably the easiest part of the process!

10. You made fun of *Bride of Godzilla*, which I have to say I think was a wise choice. The original 1955 script had an incredibly awkward line about, "It is the foreplay of love to be beaten"! You all managed to work it in there well as a joke. Was there any trepidation about working that line in there, even though it's clearly a joke?

DS: I seriously considered removing that line, but at the time it was the only line from the original story that I knew of and I wanted to keep it intact with different context. I opted to make it one of Shida's many off-the-wall comments instead, one his family could immediately call him out for. I wanted the story to feel like a fun, loving tribute to Showa-era Godzilla films, and to be respectful of the franchise without ignoring how strange the premise is, so I tried to maintain a lighthearted but not mocking tone throughout the story. In my mind, part of that meant keeping that super uncomfortable line and giving it a funnier context.

11. Again, your attention to detail and the little nuances was spot on. For instance, many of the Hong

Kong dubbers would mispronounce Godzilla as "Godziller," whose idea was it to make sure somebody did that here as well?

SS: Since this was planned as an audio experience from the start and we knew we would be producing English-language pieces, it just made sense to emulate the dubs we all grew up with and love. *Last Gargantua* was slightly unique in this sense as we actually revive a character that was originally performed in English – Russ Tamblyn's Dr. Paul Stewart from *The War of the Gargantuas*, here played very well by James Olaya. I directed James to channel Tamblyn's sleepy disinterest slightly, but inject it with gusto and charisma. I think he did very well.

DS: I knew I wanted Dr. Shida to say "Godziller" well before we heard Dan's incredible Shida audition or I'd seen anyone else's scripts. I'd decided to include it before I'd even started writing, and then discovered Raff had made the same exact same decision! We all just instinctively knew it was something that needed to be included in our scripts.

RC: I wrote "Godziller" into my script, specifically for Alex Gayhart's Doctor Yanno. Alex did such an uncanny job of sounding like a '70s international dub voice, in addition to his great overall performance. He's incredible.

12. Any plans for more audio dramas in the future?

SS: I'm a "never say never" kind of person, but at the moment there's no plans for more *Godzilla Unmade*. I'm working on more audio projects, however. Stay tuned!

LEE POWERS SKETCHBOOK

In 2019 I had the pleasure of meeting artist Lee Powers through Facebook. Lee was inspired by the many unmade Godzilla movies and began making some wonderful dioramas out of them. To date, Lee has made over a dozen and keeps on producing more! Though I would love to illustrate a future edition of *The Big Book of Japanese Giant Monster Movies: The Lost Films* with them, I cannot for legal reasons. Magazines, on the other hand, are a completely different animal legally, so I happily present them here (accompanied by my own explanations for what each of them are, and what lost film they represent). Enjoy!

One of the first unmade Godzilla movies was the aborted Americanization of *Godzilla Raids Again* (1955). The plan was to remove the Japanese cast altogether and relocate the story to America.

The new script, titled *The Volcano Monsters*, was written by Ib Melchior, and had two dinosaurs found in a Japanese volcano and transported to the U.S. There they awaken and destroy Chinatown in San Francisco (as a way of using footage of Godzilla and Anguirus battling in Osaka). The strangest part of the plan was that the dinosaurs would be just that, dinosaurs! Godzilla and Anguirus would never be named at all! The producers, AB-PT, didn't want to market the film as a sequel to *Godzilla, King of the Monsters!* (1956) at all. Godzilla would be a female Tyrannosaurus Rex out to lay eggs, and Anguirus would be a simple ankylosaur. The movie's heroes would have consisted of a military man named Steve, and elderly scientist with a heart condition, and his assistant, Marge. Two new suits of Godzilla and Anguirus (bottom inset) were constructed by Toho to fill in the script's blanks and were shipped to America and then mysteriously vanished (though, a photo exists of the American G-suit posing with the Phantom of the Opera!). When the movie was scrapped, Melchior repurposed certain elements of the plot into *Reptilicus* (1960) only a few years later.

In 1978, Nobuhiko Obayashi, the cult director of *House* (1977), pitched an insane Godzilla reboot that would reveal that Godzilla was actually a pregnant, female alien named Rozan from the Planet Godzilla! Rozan and her baby Ririn journey through space to return to Planet Godzilla, only to find it overrun by a race of aliens modeled after Egyptian mythology. The father Godzilla, Kuunin, would lead an army of Godzillas to storm the alien's palace and would defeat the main villain, General Gamoni, in outer space. At least, that's the easiest way to sum it all up. Obviously, it was far out. Though never seriously considered as a film, it was published as "A Space Godzilla" in *Starlog Magazine* in 1979.

In 1972, Toho agreed to loan Tsuburaya Productions an old suit from *Son of Godzilla* (1967) so that Tsuburaya could make their own Godzilla movie. *Godzilla vs. Redmoon* would have seen a one-eyed red dragon from the moon fly to Earth where it falls in love with a female monster, Erabus, in Okinawa. The two monsters produce a child, Halfon, who is killed by humans. The monsters ravage Okinawa, and Godzilla shows up to stop them. Supposedly, to make Redmoon, Erabus, and Halfon, they would have repurposed suits from 1972's *Daigoro vs. Goliath,* about a good orphan monster who battles a space monster. Below is Power's imagined line-up of alternate Halfon designs based on the Daigoro suit. No definite design has ever surfaced for any of the monsters.

1975's *Terror of Mechagodzilla* was meant to feature a pair of plesiosaur monsters called the Titans that fuse into the singular Titanosaurus, but were removed for the sake of the budget.

In 2015, Yukiko Takayama, screenwriter of *Terror of Mechagodzilla*, wrote a sequel story wherein Titanosaurus is resurrected as Meister-Titano (or Mecha-Titano). In the *Ghost in the Shell*-like story, Katsura Mafune (here called Lady K) is also resurrected in the year 2075 when Meister-Titano leads a robot insurrection!

An undated screenplay from the 1970s entitled *Japan S.O.S.: Godzilla's Suicide Strategy* would have seen a blind Zatoichi inspired Godzilla fight the invisible robot monster Chamelegon. No description was given for the monster other than that it would have a huge buzz saw which Powers integrated into his design at right.

Below is Power's designs for the wildest of all the unmade Godzilla reboots: *Godzilla: God's Angry Messenger*. In the apocalyptic tale, Godzilla and the Loch Ness Monster would be the engines of destruction behind *Chariots of the Gods*-inspired aliens who come to punish mankind for their wickedness!

Opposite Page: Designs of Toho's 1970s versions of *Bride of Godzilla*, of which there were three. In some there was to be a flesh and blood female Godzilla, while in others, it was a sort of female Mechagodzilla.

The Theatre of What Should Have Been
Part 1 of 3 by Stan Hyde

THE WAR OF THE WORLDS

War of the Worlds © 1953 Paramount Pictures

Written in 1898, H. G. Wells' *The War of the Worlds* initiated the 'invasion from space' genre, and has always been a story in which the most successful adaptations have been focused on the social unease and fears of the audience in the time when they were made.

Wells himself had been horrified by stories of the actions of English explorers in Tasmania. Besides overrunning the original population's hunting grounds with 200,000 sheep, the predominantly male colonialists abducted and raped native women and girls. A war between the invaders and natives, known as the 'Black War' in Australia, essentially wiped out the original Tasmanian population.

To Wells, this seemed like Darwinism in action, and presented a bleak picture of what lay in store for England, and its Empire - particularly since the military buildup of Germany seemed to be pushing the European nations toward war.

What if advanced beings arrived and treated humanity as the colonialists had treated native populations? What if the technology of the time met its match in a confrontation with a much more highly advanced species from Mars?

I think that the fears of advanced technology and the horror of being treated as a colonized population runs strongly through successful adaptations of Wells' novel, just as it had in the original novel.

New and advanced technology - in 1938 - is sometimes given as part of the explanation for one of the most infamous incidents in the history of adaptations of *The War of the Worlds*.

Orson Welles and the *Mercury Theatre on the Air* moved Wells' story to contemporary times for their radio play adaptation.

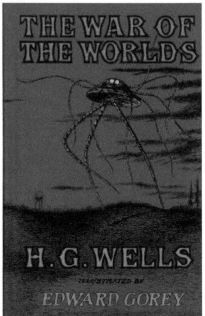

Early edition of *War of the Worlds*.

Again, as when H. G. Wells wrote the original, Germany was arming for war. Hitler had risen to power and the Nazis were on the move. (By 1933 the Nazis had established the first concentration camps for political opponents, homosexuals, and others, and more than 400 decrees and regulations had restricted aspect of the public and private lives of Germany's Jewish population). Americans felt this tension even if the country was technically practicing Isolationism at that time.

In this climate, a new technology - radio - presented Wells' story in such a way that some feel led to people being unable to tell fiction from reality (it would not be the first time that new media technology affected people this way - arguably we have still not come to terms with truth and fiction on the internet).

The War of the Worlds story was presented on air in 'breaking news'

style, with a live music broadcast interrupted by news broadcasts that report a cylindrical object landing, and later the martians appearing to use their heat-ray weapon on the crowd. A terrified reporter describes the scene until the audio feed goes dead. The story continues this way through the first half of the presentation, with various 'live reports' as the martians used weapons that mirror the fearful technologies of the period - such as the chemical weapon 'poisonous smoke' that they deploy in New York city.

The second half of the story follows a survivor - Orson Welles' narrator character - in normal radio drama style, but by then the damage was done. Though the story was clearly identified as a dramatization by *The Mercury Theatre of the Air,* many people apparently believed the show was actually happening - especially if they tuned in after the introduction and before the first commercial break 30 minutes into the show.

(It has been suggested that many people were listing to the The Chase and Sanborn Hour with Edgar Bergan and switched over to the broadcast during a musical interlude in that program. However, contemporary research shows that many of the claims of people fleeing their homes in a panic and reacting in various extreme ways up to and including suicide were exaggerated in the public outcry that followed, with news shows and newspapers inflating a story that was too good to let die. Apparently a national radio survey was being held that night and only 2 percent of listens said they were listening to Orson Wells or the Mercury Theatre, with none replying that they were listening to a live broadcast. The Myth Of the War of the Worlds Panic: https://slate.com/culture/2013/10/orson-welles-war-of-the-worlds-panic-myth-the-infamous-radio-broadcast-did-not-cause-a-nationwide-hysteria.html)

Joseph Sargent's film *The Night That Panicked America* (1975) with a script by Nicholas Meyer particularly focused on the idea that it was the relatively new medium of radio that was at the root of the panic. In that film, direct connections are made to Hitler's use of new media to influence the Nazi rise to power. *The Night That Panicked America* was broadcast on October 31st, 1975, Halloween, while the Welles broadcast was aired on October 30th, 1938 - also in honour of Halloween.

Record release of the original broadcast. Following two page spread: Artwork from the first edition of the novel.

Besides promoting a legend of panic in the newspapers, the Welles broadcast also reminded film producers that *The War of the Worlds* could, if handled right, cause a frenzy at the cinema box office too. The film rights had been held by Paramount since the silent movie days, and various attempts to launch the project had failed (more on that in a moment), but at least the broadcast did launch the directing career of Orson Welles, who declined to ever be involved in a film adaptation of *The War of the Worlds*, but did get the opportunity to make *Citizen Kane* (1941).

Just as the novel and the radio broadcast associated contemporary events with alien invasion, the two most successful film adaptations exploited the audience' current fears.

George Pal's *The War of the Worlds* (1953) film is set in California, instead of the England of the novel, and is given a much more contemporary Cold War feeling in line with the tensions the audience felt at the time. Even the pre-title montage develops this theme, showcasing the evolution of destruction in a sequence that ends tellingly with the launch of a V-2 missile.

Paul Frees tells us, "In the first World War, and for the first time in the history of man, nations combined to fight against nations using the crude weapons of those days. The second World War involved every continent on the globe, and men turned to science for new devices of warfare, which reached an unparalleled peak in their capacity for destruction. And now, fought with the terrible weapons of super-science, menacing all mankind and every creature on Earth, comes...The War of the Worlds!"

In terms of the story, Gene Barry's Dr. Clayton Forrester (er, no relation to *Mystery Science Theatre's* Dr. Clayton Forrester . . . at least I don't think so) experiences a number of the events similar to those Wells' novel, hiding in a destroyed house, a close encounter with a martian, and being reunited with his love - in this case the lovely Ann Robinson as Sylvia van Buren.

However, the character he plays is much more in tune with the Cold War 50's, not a writer as in Wells' book, but a scientist whose work with Pacific Tech is vital to the resistance to the martians, and who is shown consulting with the United States Marine Corps as if the military consulting scientists was a routine event. This is similar to other SF films of the time like *The Thing From Another World* (1951) and much of the plot is focused on scientific endeavour in an attempt to beat the martians at their own game (at least until our most powerful weapon, the atomic bomb, is tried and fails to stop them). In all these respects it's a story of its time.

Skipping ahead to Steven Spielberg's 2005 *The War of The Worlds*, again the politics of the time was important. While David Koepp says that he did not want to put in explicit references to September 11 or the Iraq War, he did say that the scene where Tom Cruise's son abandons the family to join the forces confronting the alien was inspired by teenagers fighting in the Gaza Strip. "I was thinking of teenagers in Gaza throwing bottles and rocks at tanks, and I think that when you're that age you don't fully consider the ramifications of what you're doing and you're very much caught up in the moment and passion, whether that's a good idea or not."

Like Wells' original novel, contemporary fears seemed paramount in the film and Spielberg does admit that reflecting post 911 fears was a conscious subtext he was developing.

From scenes in which Tom Cruise's character Ray Ferrier washes off the ash created by the alien's destruction of buildings and people (is it a baptism in which he is reborn as a father?), to waking up to a crashed airplane that has destroyed the neighbourhood - and any sense of normality - in which his ex-wife lives, the journey of the main character often mirrors the horrific incidents inspired by 911. Rachel Ferrier (Dakota Fanning) even asks, "Is that the terrorists?" as they escape New York. Home-made missing person posters line the streets as the family approaches the ferry.

At the same time, misgivings about the Iraq War seem to be part of the subtext too. Just as Wells' original novel was inspired by misgivings about the actions of the English colonials, anxiety about America's role as an occupying force seem to drive some of the imagery as well.

Ray Ferrier's son, Robbie Ferrier (Justin Chatwin) is working on an essay about the French occupation of Algeria, notably the inspiration for the famous film *The Battle of Algiers* which focus on the guerrilla movement by the Algerians and the torture and other illegal methods used by colonial powers to subdue the uprising. Tim Robbins' survivalist character Harlan Ogilvy (a combination of the several characters from the original novel) says, "We're the resistance, Ray. Occupation has always failed. History's taught us that a thousand times."

Finally, when the martians are felled by tiny bacteria, and a fallen martian tripod martian is first seen by Ray when he is standing beside a Minute Man in Boston, again underscoring the idea of resistance to a force from outside. The images have a double-meaning, under-scoring both the need to rise up against invasion from the outside, and a warning about the dangers of becoming the invader yourself.

Besides allegory, the film has many references to the George Pal film, from the energy shields that protect the Martian war machines to a cameo by Gene Barry (Dr. Clayton Forrester) and Ann Robinson (Sylvia van Buren) - the stars of the original *The War of the Worlds* -as the parents of Ray's wife at the end of the film.

As we will see, the George Pal film remains incredibly influential both in completed and unmade versions of the story.

THE LOST FILMS

The film rights for *The War of the Worlds* were initially purchased in perpetuity for Cecil B. DeMille in 1925. (This was actually problematic later, for when the George Pal film went into production Paramount discovered they had only purchased the silent film rights, and a deal had to be negotiated with Wells' estate for the rights to a sound film.)

DeMille was apparently attracted to the story of large scale destruction. The film was seen as a follow-up to his very successful 1923 version of 'The Ten Commandments.'

The *New York Times* leaked a story that Arzen Doscerepy, a famous German Technical expert, had been hired to complete the film's special effects. Apparently he had 'spent two years perfecting devices and mechanism which will make Wells' martians walk and spray death around the world.' Doscrerepy's work was apparently 'very similar' to the stop-motion animation that Willis O'Brien had employed to make dinosaurs come to life in *The Lost World* (1925).

As well, the film was to be shot partially in the 2-strip Technicolor process, alternated with black and white.

Unlike later successful versions of the tale, writer Roy Pomeroy's script for the movie was more focused on characters and less on the fears of contemporary audiences, and this may have resulted in DeMille losing interest in the project. The focus of the story was a love triangle between socialite Celia, Freeman Jones (the Secretary of National Defense, who is oddly also a pacifist), and inventor Robert Eliot. Forgoing the simple story from the book of the narrator searching for his wife amid the destruction was probably a mistake.

Communication has been established with a civilization on Mars. As the scene opens at a dinner party, Jones is explaining why he will not provide any more money for armaments, to Celia, who is not happy to be at the party. Her true love is inventor Robert Eliot, who is home from the party working on his inventions.

Elsewhere, Robert is terrifying his landlady with his death ray. He quells the woman's fears by explaining that he has also created a counter-device that turns the ray back on its source.

(With its love triangle and super-science weapons, the set-up bears a bit of a resemblance to the plot of the original *Gojira* [1954].)

Robert accidentally destroys his death-ray when he aims it at the reflector. Oops! - so much for the only working model of his work.

A meteor crashes to earth, startling the guests at the party.

The next day, newspapers are headlining the fall of huge metal cylinders all over the U.S. (DeMille's invasion was limited to the U.S.A., just as Wells' original novel was limited to the United Kingdom.)

Freeman Jones continues to disregard the danger, saying, "People will believe anything if they were less ignorant they would know that this is the season in which, for thousands of years, meteorites have fallen to the Earth."

Elliot comes to Jones' office to attempt to finance the death ray and reflector. At first Jones is simply bored, but when he realizes that this is the man Celia is infatuated with, he turns openly hostile. He will never spend taxpayer money on lunatic ideas.

The argument is interrupted when a cylinder smashes against the building. The invaders begin their assault by using poisonous gas to kill the population of Washington. Everyone flees - except Celia who tries to wait for Eliot.

Her father finds her and carries her off. Eliot follows her to the country.

Another meteor crash has separated Celia from her family, and, while lost in the woods, she comes across a trail of phosphorescence. She spots the creature that is leaving the trail, it is three feet high and waddles on short, fin-like legs. It looks at her with its vile semblance of a human face and she almost faints in horror.

Eliot rescues her and together they examine a nearby fallen cylinder. At this point the fighting machines with their heat rays emerge ("strange and weird airships moving like immense vultures"). Subsequently there are battles with planes and mobile railroad artillery. New York is attacked, the Atlantic Fleet is obliterated, and destruction is widespread as the 'hideous gnomes' ride their tripods in an orgy of destruction

Eliot and Celia learn the truth behind the martian plan. They are looking for beautiful Earth women with whom they plan to breed and propagate a mixed Martian-Earth race to populate the conquered Earth with.

(Shades of *The Mysterians* [1957]. Though in 1925 the first science fiction pulp magazine *Amazing Stories* was a year away, and even the word science fiction had not yet been coined - it would be 'scientifiction' in Amazing for years yet . . . it is surprising that DeMille's main plot, bug-eyed monsters abducting our women, raised it's head at the very beginning of the genre's history. The notion would be used to sell pulp magazines and exploitation films for many years to come.)

Eliot and Celia escape to New York's subway tunnels, finding a band of refugees lead by Freeman Jones. Feeling flush with power as the leader of the refugees, Jones attempts to rape Celia, chasing her down an abandoned tunnel.

Meanwhile, Eliot has found a scientific colleague and together they start to build the death-ray reflector. (Yes, Eliot's original invention is the very thing that the martians are using to devastate the U.S.A.)

Celia's escape is interrupted by the Martians, who capture her with a "huge mechanical claw." The horrified Freeman Jones flees.

Eliot meanwhile has completed the death-ray reflector and, when Jones returns, implores him to get his band of refugees to move the device to the surface. Jones refuses. Eliot's friend hits him in the head and then the two men get the device to the surface with the help of the other men.

Jones makes another attempt to destroy the reflector (by this time one really has to question his motives) but a Martian ray disintegrates him. (At last!)

Meanwhile the resistance army drags the reflector from place to place, destroying the martian machines. ("*The Martians seem very slow to catch on to what's happening.*" Bill Warren observes, in his great *Keep Watching the Skies* history of science fiction films.)

Celia is saved from the 'fate worse than death' when the passionate Martian gnome who has captured her notices that his comrades are being destroyed all around him. At first he joins the battle, but as the tide turns he flees, pursued by Eliot.

His tripod machine comes to a stop at a river, the Martian unsure about which direction to take to escape. In the meantime, Eliot hesitates to use the reflector, worried that he will kill Celia.

Not to worry. The Martian war machine has sunk in the soft river mud and becomes immobile. The Martian realizes this, abandons his machine, and immediately drowns. (No swimming lessons on Mars I guess?)

Eliot saves Celia. Congratulations all around.

The story outline concludes: "*The sun rises on a later day, over the reconstructed cities of America, into the air swarming with aerial traffic. Eliot and Celia come out on the bright, angular, but beautiful rooftop portico of their skyscraper palace. With their beautiful Earthchildren . . . they sit down to breakfast in the warm, wholesome sunshine of a New America.*"

DeMille apparently lost interest in the project and moved on to other movies.

It's easy to see why. The single-minded drive of the novel, with it's straight-forward attempt to re-unite the narrator with his wife as the simple thread that drives the

Cecil B. Demille, the man who almost made *War of the Worlds.*

story, has been lost in a meandering plot that throws a lot of the villainy in the director of the human character Freeman Jones.

He seems like a major a distraction from the real villains, and one wonders if some of this is in the script to hedge a bet in case the special effect proved problematic (1925's *The Lost World* is similarly over-scripted in terms of the human characters 'just in case' the effects proved problematic.)

And of course the focus on aliens (outsiders, immigrants, what-have-you) who *want our women* if not yet a cliche, is still silly.

It's fascinating to wonder if the appearance of *The War of the Worlds* in 1926, alongside 1925's *The Lost World* and 1927's *Metropolis* might have started a vogue for science fiction in the 1930's instead of the 1950's. But that was not to be, and maybe we're all the better for it, since Universal's gothic revival of the 1930's might never have happened. In any case, this version of *The War of the Worlds* is an interesting product of its times, but I can't say I'm very sad it was never made.

The story stayed in development hell at Paramount for the next 28 years. When Jesse L. Lasky, the man who produced Hollywood's first feature film, DeMille's *The Squaw Man* (1913) (in a barn) gained control of Paramount he decided that *The War of the Worlds* could be a great success.

Lasky offered the great Russian director, Sergei Eisenstein (*Battleship Potemkin* [1925]) an opportunity to make a film in the United States. Arriving in May 1930, one of the projects that was offered to him was *The War Of The Worlds*. Though work on another script was begun, the pre-production dragged on and Eisenstein withdrew to complete a script for Theodore Dreiser's *An American Tragedy*. Apparently Lasky ultimately shelved the alien invasion project at that time, deciding it was impossible to make because of all the special photography required.

By late October 1930, Eisenstein was on his way back to Moscow. The script for *An American Tragedy* had not pleased Paramount, and worse yet, Major Frank Pease, the president of the Hollywood Technical Director's Institute and anti-communist, had mounted a public campaign against Eisenstein which frankly worried Paramount. On October 23, 1930 the two parties declared their contract 'null and void' and Eisenstein and some of the technical assistants he had brought with him were on the boat back to Moscow via tickets bought for them by Paramount

This ends a fascinating period in the development of *The War of the Worlds* in terms of the film-makers involved with it. Cecile B. DeMille and Sergei Eisenstein are probably the two men most associated with the creation of the most influential two styles of editing used in motion pictures.

DeMille started in the industry before the role of editor existed, and cut his films in such a way that the audience did not notice the cuts, hiding them as natural breaks in the flow of action. This *continuity editing* style is what we generally expect in narrative films, and it creates a smooth flow of narrative and enhances emotional impact in a way that is very theatrical. (In later years, DeMille would allow his editors to assemble the cut on their own, but would then screen the footage and give suggestions for improvement.)

On the other hand Eisenstein is the father of ideological montage in which an image creates conflict with another image, thus creating contrasting ideas in the minds of the audience.

He identified five kinds of montage, and though there isn't time to cover them all, it is fascinating to think what a contrast his film would have been to DeMille's. I imagine it would have been closer to Wells' novel, since that would have better fit his style, and that the contemporary political situation (with Germany once again building up to war and unrest in the Soviet Union and around the world) would have played a bigger part in the film.

Eisenstein's montage idea (sometimes called 'soviet montage') is what Alfred Hitchcock also called 'pure film.' (His example was a shot of a man staring, and then a second shot of the man slightly smiling. If another shot is placed between them - say a mother and child - the man seems to become likeable, the slight smile triggered by the remembrance of the joy of parenthood. On the other hand, if instead of a mother and child the in-between shot is a girl in a bikini . . . we react to the man as if he is a pervert. That's the power of montage/pure film.)

Speaking of Alfred Hitchcock, apparently he approached Wells personally in Nice in 1934 to try to convince him he should be allowed to make a film version.

At the time Hitchcock was well known in England, but not yet known in the United States. Apparently Wells liked Hitchcock's ideas for the film, but told him that the novel was owned in perpetuity by Paramount. Also around this time, and again no-doubt a victim of Paramount's ownership of rights, Alexander Korda thought of making the film of *The War of the Worlds*, but ultimately settled on making Wells' *Things to Come*(1936) with a script by Wells himself. (Korda also made Wells' *The Man Who Could Work Miracles* again released in 1936 with participation by Wells in the script-writing)

In 1935, the *New York Times* printed a story focused on Wally Westmore, makeup chief at Paramount, who was apparently sketching out ideas for the martians. The story explained, "Westmore thinks they ought to be ghastly white with black trimmings - so as to give the customers a jolt for their money." No director for the adaptation is mentioned in the article.

Some sources claim that Paramount pressured Wells to make *The War of the Worlds* his first feature film, after his famous broadcast in 1938 made him notorious. However, Bill Warren in *'Keep Watching the Skies'* thinks this this is unlikely, since it was RKO that brought him out to Hollywood and not Paramount. This seems pretty reasonable to me.

According to Warren, Hollywood trade announced that Paramount was preparing *The War of the Worlds* in 1940. Probably inspired by the radio broadcast, nothing came of this attempt either.

To be continued next issue (including the Ray Harryhausen version and an axed TV series!!!)

THE BICEP BOOKS CATALOGUE

The following titles are available for purchase on Amazon.com, and are available to bookstores at a wholesale discount via Ingram Content Group (ISBNs of available editions listed for this purpose)

THE BIG BOOK OF JAPANESE GIANT MONSTER MOVIES SERIES

The third edition of the book that started it all! Reviews over 100 tokusatsu films between 1954 and 1988. All the Godzilla, Gamera, and Daimajin movies made during the Showa era are covered plus lesser known fare like *Invisible Man vs. The Human Fly* (1957) and *Conflagration* (1975). Softcover (380 pp/5.83" X 8.27") Suggested Retail: $19.99 ISBN: 978-1-7341546-4-1

This third edition reviews over 75 tokusatsu films between 1989 and 2019. All the Godzilla, Gamera, and Ultraman movies made during the Heisei era are covered plus independent films like *Reigo, King of the Sea Monsters* and *Attack of the Giant Teacher*! Softcover (260 pp/5.83" X 8.27") Suggested Retail: $19.99 ISBN: 978-1-7347816-4-9

Covering unproduced scripts like *Bride of Godzilla* (1955), partially shot movies like *Giant Horde Beast Nezura* (1963), and banned films like *Prophecies of Nostradamus* (1974), this second edition of the Rondo Award nominated book covers hundreds of lost productions. 470 pp. Softcover/Hardcover (7" X 10") Suggested Retail: $24.99(sc)/$39.95(hc) ISBN: 978-1-7341546-0-3 (hc)

This sequel to *The Lost Films* covers the non-giant monster unmade movie scripts from Japan such as *Frankenstein vs. the Human Vapor* (1963), *After Japan Sinks* (1974-76), plus lost movies like *Fearful Attack of the Flying Saucers* (1956) and *Venus Flytrap* (1968). Hardcover (200 pp/5.83" X 8.27")/Softcover (216 pp/5.5" X 8.5") Suggested Retail: $9.99 (sc)/$24.99(hc) ISBN: 978-1-7341546-3-4 (hc)

This companion book to *The Lost Films* charts the development of all the prominent Japanese monster movies including discarded screenplays, story ideas, and deleted scenes. Also includes bios for writers like Shinichi Sekizawa, Niisan Takahashi and many others. Comprehensive script listing and appendices as well. Hardcover/Softcover (370 pp./6" X 9") Suggested Retail: $16.95(sc)/$34.99(hc) ISBN: 978-1-7341546-5-8 (hc)

Throughout the 1960s and 1970s the Italian film industry cranked out over 600 "Spaghetti Westerns" and for every *Fistful of Dollars* were a dozen pale imitations, some of them hilarious. Many of these lesser known Spaghettis are available in bargain bin DVD packs and stream for free online. If ever you've wondered which are worth your time and which aren't, this is the book for you. Softcover (160pp./5.06" X 7.8") Suggested Retail: $9.99

THE BICEP BOOKS CATALOGUE

MOVIES UNMADE SERIES

Kong Unmade explores unproduced scripts like *King Kong vs. Frankenstein* (1958), unfinished films like *The Lost Island* (1934), and lost movies like *King Kong Appears in Edo* (1938). As a bonus, all the Kong rip-offs like *Konga* (1961) and *Queen Kong* (1976) are reviewed. Hardcover (350 pp/5.83" X 8.27")/Softcover (376 pp/5.5" X 8.5") Suggested Retail: $24.99(hc)/$19.99 (sc) ISBN: 978-1-7341546-2-7(hc)

Jaws Unmade explores unproduced scripts like *Jaws 3, People 0* (1979), abandoned ideas like a Quint prequel, and even aborted sequels to Jaws inspired movies like *Orca Part II*. As a bonus, all the Jaws rip-offs like *Grizzly* (1976) and *Tentacles* (1977) are reviewed. Hardcover (316 pp/5.83" X 8.27")/Softcover (340 pp/5.5" X 8.5") Suggested Retail: $29.99(hc)/$17.95 (sc) ISBN: 978-1-7344730-1-8(hc)

Coming in 2021, *Classic Monsters Unmade* will cover lost and unmade films starring Dracula, Frankenstein, the Mummy and more monsters from Universal, Hammer, and beyond. Covers everything from *The Wolf Man vs. Dracula* to *Frankenstein vs. Godzilla*. Alternate versions of completed movies like *Frankenstein Meets the Wolfman* and *Horror of Dracula* will also be covered.

NOSTALGIA

Written at an intermediate reading level for the kid in all of us, these picture books will take you back to your youth. In the spirit of the old Ian Thorne books are covered *Giant Apes of the Movies, Dinosauruses of the Movies* and *Monster Insects of the Movies*.

Hardcover/Softcover (44 pp/7.5" X 9.25") Suggested Retail: $17.95(hc)/ $9.99(sc) ISBN: 978-1-7341546-9-6 (hc) 978-1-7344730-5-6 (sc)

Hardcover/Softcover (44 pp/7.5" X 9.25") Suggested Retail: $17.95(hc)/ $9.99(sc) ISBN: 978-1-7344730-6-3 (hc) 978-1-7344730-7-0 (sc)

Hardcover/Softcover (44 pp/7.5" X 9.25") Suggested Retail: $17.95(hc)/ $9.99(sc) ISBN: 978-1-7347816-3-2 (hc) 978-1-7347816-2-5(sc)

THE BICEP BOOKS CATALOGUE

CRYPTOZOOLOGY/COWBOYS & SAURIANS

Cowboys & Saurians: Prehistoric Beasts as Seen by the Pioneers explores dinosaur sightings from the pioneer period via real newspaper reports from the time. Well-known cases like the Tombstone Thunderbird are covered along with more obscure cases like the Crosswicks Monster and more. Softcover (357 pp/5.06" X 7.8") Suggested Retail: $19.95 ISBN: 978-1-7341546-1-0

Cowboys & Saurians: Ice Age zeroes in on snowbound saurians like the Ceratosaurus of the Arctic Circle and a Tyrannosaurus of the Tundra, as well as sightings of Ice Age megafauna like mammoths, glyptodonts, Sarkastodons and Saber-toothed tigers. Tales of a land that time forgot in the Arctic are also covered. Softcover (264 pp/5.06" X 7.8") Suggested Retail: $14.99 ISBN: 978-1-7341546-7-2

Southerners & Saurians takes the series formula of exploring newspaper accounts of monsters in the pioneer period with an eye to the Old South. In addition to dinosaurs are covered Lizardmen, Frogmen, giant leeches and mosquitoes, and the Dingocroc, which might be an alien rather than a prehistoric survivor. Softcover (202 pp/5.06" X 7.8") Suggested Retail: $13.99 ISBN: 978-1-7344730-4-9

UFOLOGY/THE REAL COWBOYS & ALIENS IN CONJUNCTION WITH ROSWELL BOOKS

The Real Cowboys and Aliens: Early American UFOs explores UFO sightings in the USA between the years 1899-1864. Stories of encounters sometimes involved famous figures in U.S. history such as Lewis and Clark, and Thomas Jefferson. Hardcover (242pp/6" X 9") Softcover (262 pp/5.06" X 7.8") Suggested Retail: $24.99 (hc)/$15.95(sc) ISBN: 978-1-7341546-8-9 (hc)/978-1-7344730-8-7 (sc)

The second entry in the series, *Old West UFOs*, covers reports spanning the years 1865-1895. Includes tales of Men in Black, Reptilians, Spring-Heeled Jack, Sasquatch from space, and other alien beings, in addition to the UFOs and airships. Hardcover (276 pp/6" X 9") Softcover (308 pp/5.06" X 7.8") Suggested Retail: $29.95 (hc)/$17.95 (sc) ISBN: 978-1-7344730-0-1 (hc)/ 978-1-7344730-2-5 (sc)

The third entry in the series, *The Coming of the Airships*, encompasses a short time frame with an incredibly high concentration of airship sightings between 1896-1899. The famous Aurora, Texas, UFO crash of 1897 is covered in depth along with many others. Hardcover (196 pp/6" X 9") Softcover (222 pp/5.06" X 7.8") Suggested Retail: $24.99 (hc)/$15.95 (sc) ISBN: 978-1-7347816-1-8 (hc)/ 978-1-7347816-0-1(sc)

BACK ISSUES

THE LOST FILMS FANZINE

ISSUE #1 SPRING 2020 The lost Italian cut of *Legend of Dinosaurs and Monster Birds* called *Terremoto 10 Grado*, plus *Bride of Dr. Phibes* script, *Good Luck! Godzilla*, the King Kong remake that became a car comm ercial, Bollywood's lost *Jaws* rip-off, Top Ten Best Fan Made Godzilla trailers plus an interview with Scott David Lister. 60 pages. Three variant covers/editions (premium color/basic color/b&w)

ISSUE #2 SUMMER 2020 How 1935's *The Capture of Tarzan* became 1936's *Tarzan Escapes*, the Orca sequels that weren't, Baragon in Bollywood's *One Million B.C.*, unmade *Kolchak: The Night Stalker* movies, *The Norliss Tapes*, *Superman V: The New Movie*, why there were no *Curse of the Pink Panther* sequels, *Moonlight Mask: The Movie*. 64 pages. Two covers/editions (basic color/b&w)

ISSUE #3 FALL 2020 Blob sequels both forgotten and unproduced, *Horror of Dracula* uncut, *Frankenstein Meets the Wolfman* and talks, myths of the lost *King Kong* Spider-Pit sequence debunked, the *Carnosaur* novel vs. the movies, *Terror in the Streets* 50th anniversary, *Bride of Godzilla* 55th Unniversary, Lee Powers sketchbook. 100 pages. Two covers/editions (basic color/b&w)

MOVIE MILESTONES

ISSUE #1 AUGUST 2020 Debut issue celebrating 80 years of *One Million B.C.* (1940), and an early 55th Anniversary for *One Million Years B.C.* (1966). Abandoned ideas, casting changes, and deleted scenes are covered, plus, a mini-B.C. stock-footage filmography and much more! Three collectible covers/editions (premium color/basic color/b&w)

ISSUE #2 OCTOBER 2020 Celebrates the joint 50th Anniversaries of *When Dinosaurs Ruled the Earth* (1970) and *Creatures the World Forgot* (1971). Also includes looks at *Prehistoric Women* (1967), *When Women Had Tails* (1970), and *Caveman* (1981), plus unmade films like *When the World Cracked Open*. Three collectible covers/editions (premium color/basic color/b&w)

COMING SOON ISSUE #3 TBD 2021 This issue will celebrate the joint 60th Anniversaries of *Gorgo*, *Reptilicus* and *Konga* examining unmade sequels like *Reptilicus 2*, and other related lost projects like *Kuru Island* and *The Volcano Monsters*. More content TBD. Three collectible covers/editions (premium color/basic color/b&w)

NEXT ISSUE

The December issue will have a bad case of the 'D's with *Diamonds Are Forever's* first draft (starring Goldfinger!), *Death Wish 6: The New Vigilante*, *The Day the Earth Stood Still 2*, and Hammer's *Disciple of Dracula*!!! Stan Hyde's fascinating look at *War of the Worlds* adaptations that weren't continue, Patrick Galvan examines *Spring Dream in the Old Capital*, and more!!!

MAD SCIENTIST

Issue 1   **May 2000**

**MARVEL COMICS'
GODZILLA!**

**CRUSH, CRUMBLE,
& CHOMP!**

**THE FLESH
EATERS!**

Look for a 20th Anniversary issue from Martin Arlt soon!
www.madscientistzine.com

BE SURE TO LISTEN TO

Join hosts Byrd and Matt as they discuss all things giant monsters, tokusatsu, and Japanese fantasy films. We'll also cover comics, cartoons, toys, books, and more! Come here for a regular dose of everything from Godzilla and Gamera to King Kong and Ray Harryhausen to Ultraman, and everything in between!

CPSIA information can be obtained
at www.ICGtesting.com
Printed in the USA
LVHW071453221020
669279LV00017B/619

9 781734 781670